영문법 판매 1위, 중학영문법 3800제의 초등시리즈

초등영문법 3800제

LEVEL 1

입문 1 단계

발행 초판 22쇄(2024년 8월 31일)
책임편집 서은숙 **편집** 성은혜 **원고집필** 정다혜, 권은정, 김주현, 정은주, 김유미, 홍주희 **연습문제집필** 조윤경, 권은정, 김송이, 김주희
워크북집필 윤정한, 정다혜, 김주희, 김송이 **원고검토** 유예슬, 최희찬, 박문정, 백경빈, 김미경, 김규은, 양원석, 고민정 **영문감수** Kathryn O'Handley
감수 오현진(강남구청 중등인강 강사) **교정** 황희진, 정다혜, 김주희, 이은영, 하은옥, 홍성경, 오정훈, 심가원, 이은혜, 신영은, 김송이, 하새롬
베타테스트 신재진, 이옥현, 유윤정, 정요한, 신소미, 장신혜, 변선영, 정은주
녹음 와이알 미디어 **녹음대본정리** 신소미, 김소정, 김건탁, 김윤아, 최안나 **녹음검수** 이상미, 신소미, 김소정, 김주희, 윤수경, 이옥현, 이유진, 최안나
사진검색 신의진, 김윤아, 이은혜, 손주연 **삽화** 박현주 **표지디자인** 김연실 **인디자인편집** 정은영, 박정민, 박경아, 김미라, 고연화
제작 이주영 **발행처** ㈜마더텅 **발행인** 문숙영 **주소** 서울시 금천구 가마산로 96, 708호

MOTHERTONGUE
마더텅출판사
since1999.4.1.

이렇게 공부하세요.

LEVEL 1

STEP 1

문법 개념을 익힌 후 확인테스트를 풀어보면서 제대로 이해했는지 확인해요.

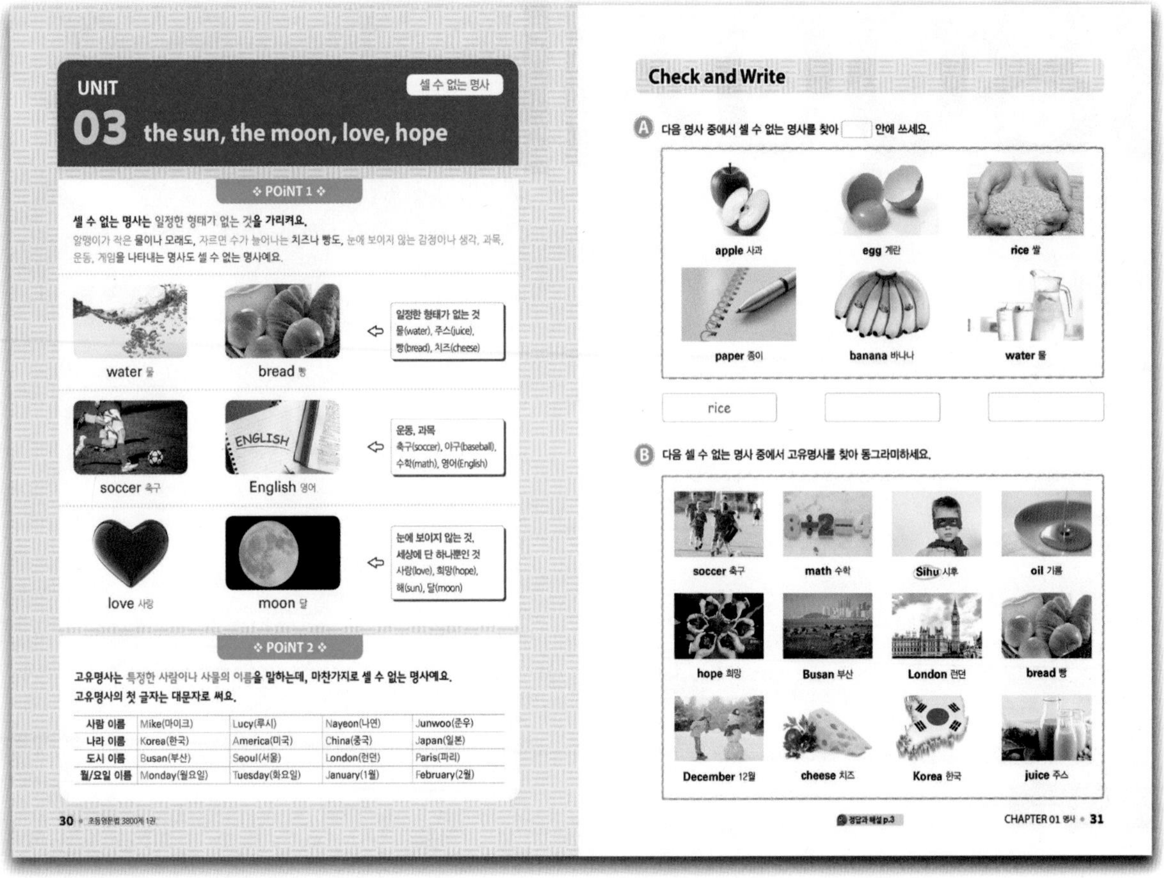
UNIT 03 the sun, the moon, love, hope
셀 수 없는 명사

POiNT 1

셀 수 없는 명사는 일정한 형태가 없는 것을 가리켜요.
알갱이가 작은 물이나 모래도, 자르면 수가 늘어나는 치즈나 빵도, 눈에 보이지 않는 감정이나 생각, 과목, 운동, 게임을 나타내는 명사도 셀 수 없는 명사예요.

water 물 / bread 빵 ⇦ 일정한 형태가 없는 것 물(water), 주스(juice), 빵(bread), 치즈(cheese)

soccer 축구 / English 영어 ⇦ 운동, 과목 축구(soccer), 야구(baseball), 수학(math), 영어(English)

love 사랑 / moon 달 ⇦ 눈에 보이지 않는 것, 세상에 단 하나뿐인 것 사랑(love), 희망(hope), 해(sun), 달(moon)

POiNT 2

고유명사는 특정한 사람이나 사물의 이름을 말하는데, 마찬가지로 셀 수 없는 명사예요.
고유명사의 첫 글자는 대문자로 써요.

사람 이름	Mike(마이크)	Lucy(루시)	Nayeon(나연)	Junwoo(준우)
나라 이름	Korea(한국)	America(미국)	China(중국)	Japan(일본)
도시 이름	Busan(부산)	Seoul(서울)	London(런던)	Paris(파리)
월/요일 이름	Monday(월요일)	Tuesday(화요일)	January(1월)	February(2월)

30 초등영문법 3800제 1권

Check and Write

A 다음 명사 중에서 셀 수 없는 명사를 찾아 안에 쓰세요.

apple 사과 / egg 계란 / rice 쌀 / paper 종이 / banana 바나나 / water 물

rice

B 다음 셀 수 없는 명사 중에서 고유명사를 찾아 동그라미하세요.

soccer 축구 / math 수학 / Sihu 시후 / oil 기름 / hope 희망 / Busan 부산 / London 런던 / bread 빵 / December 12월 / cheese 치즈 / Korea 한국 / juice 주스

정답과 해설 p.3 CHAPTER 01 명사 31

STEP 2

Practice 1, 2, 3

Practice 1, 2, 3로 구성된 연습문제를 풀면서 앞에서 배운 문법이 적용된 풍부한 예문을 접할 수 있어요. 연습 문제들을 풀다보면, 서술형 문제도 더 이상 어렵지 않아요!

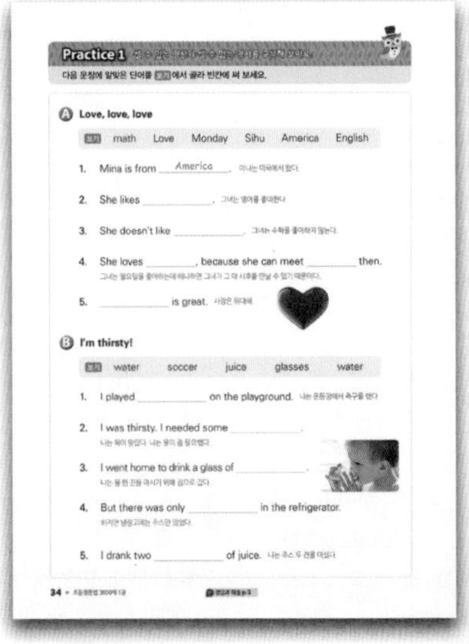
Practice 1
A Love, love, love
math Love Monday Sihu America English
1. Mina is from America.
2. She likes ______.
3. She doesn't like ______.
4. She loves ______, because she can meet ______ then.
5. ______ is great.
B I'm thirsty!
water soccer juice glasses water
1. I played ______ on the playground.
2. I was thirsty. I needed some ______.
3. I went home to drink a glass of ______.
4. But there was only ______ in the refrigerator.
5. I drank two ______ of juice.
34

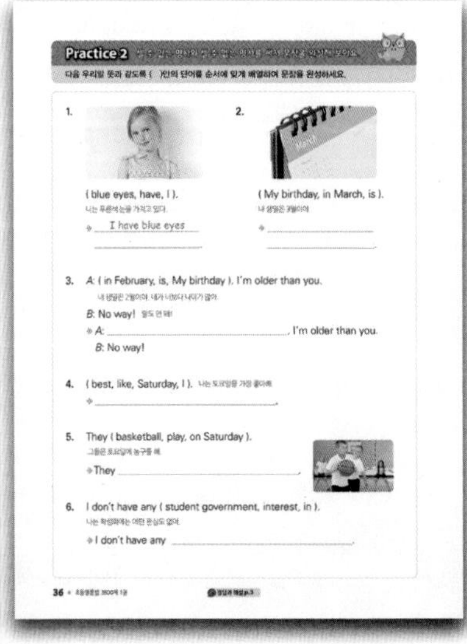
Practice 2
1. (blue eyes, have, I). I have blue eyes
2. (My birthday, in March, is).
3. A: (in February, is, My birthday). I'm older than you.
B: No way!
4. (best, like, Saturday, I).
5. They (basketball, play, on Saturday).
6. I don't have any (student government, interest, in).
36

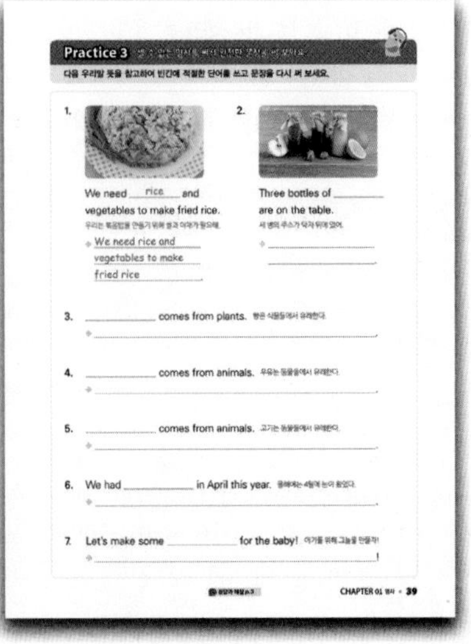
Practice 3
1. We need rice and vegetables to make fried rice.
2. Three bottles of ______ are on the table.
3. ______ comes from plants.
4. ______ comes from animals.
5. ______ comes from animals.
6. We had ______ in April this year.
7. Let's make some ______ for the baby!
CHAPTER 01 명사 39

STEP 3

Let's Practice More!

문법 내용을 제대로 이해했는지 확인할 수 있도록 SET 01–08까지 다양한 유형의 연습문제를 실었어요.
문제를 하나하나 풀다보면 해당 UNIT의 핵심 개념을 제대로 익히게 될 거에요.

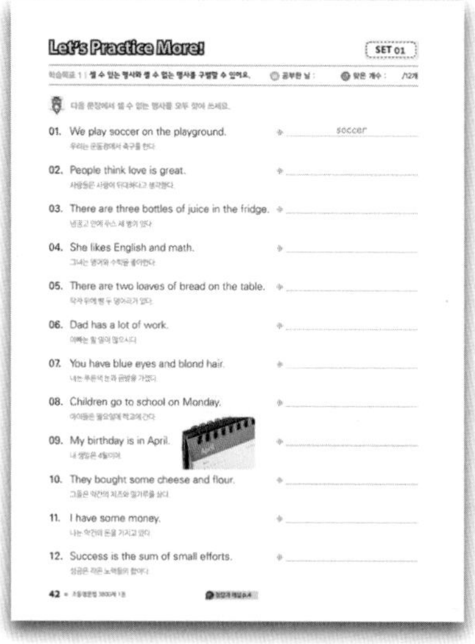
Let's Practice More! SET 01

01. We play soccer on the playground. → soccer
02. People think love is great.
03. There are three bottles of juice in the fridge.
04. She likes English and math.
05. There are two loaves of bread on the table.
06. Dad has a lot of work.
07. You have blue eyes and blond hair.
08. Children go to school on Monday.
09. My birthday is in April.
10. They bought some cheese and flour.
11. I have some money.
12. Success is the sum of small efforts.

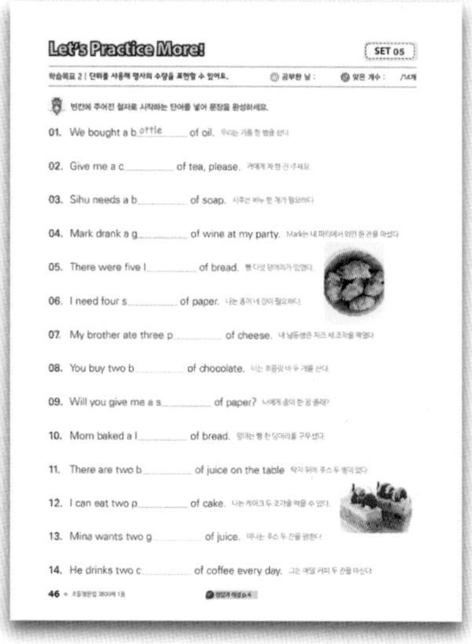
Let's Practice More! SET 05

01. We bought a b<u>ottle</u> of oil.
02. Give me a c______ of tea, please.
03. Sihu needs a b______ of soap.
04. Mark drank a g______ of wine at my party.
05. There were five l______ of bread.
06. I need four s______ of paper.
07. My brother ate three p______ of cheese.
08. You buy two b______ of chocolate.
09. Will you give me a s______ of paper?
10. Mom baked a l______ of bread.
11. There are two b______ of juice on the table.
12. I can eat two p______ of cake.
13. Mina wants two g______ of juice.
14. He drinks two c______ of coffee every day.

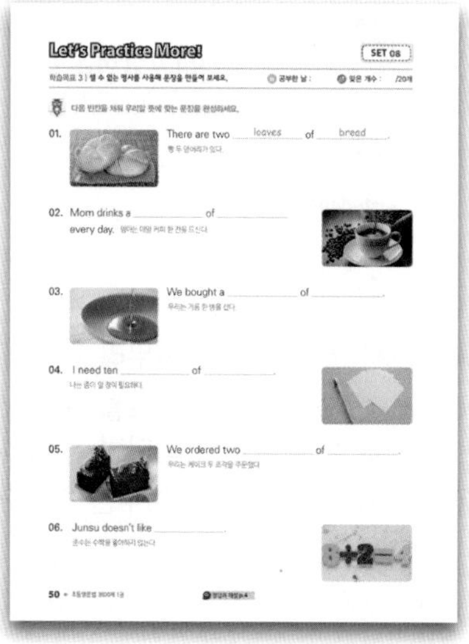
Let's Practice More! SET 08

01. There are two <u>loaves</u> of <u>bread</u>.
02. Mom drinks a ______ of ______ every day.
03. We bought a ______ of ______.
04. I need ten ______ of ______.
05. We ordered two ______ of ______.
06. Junsu doesn't like ______.

STEP 4

마무리 실전테스트

최종 마무리 테스트로서 권당 2회분의 실전테스트를 실었어요. 총 30문제의 진단평가 및
교내평가 유형의 실전문제로 앞에서 배운 내용을 복습하고 취약한 부분을 파악해 봐요.

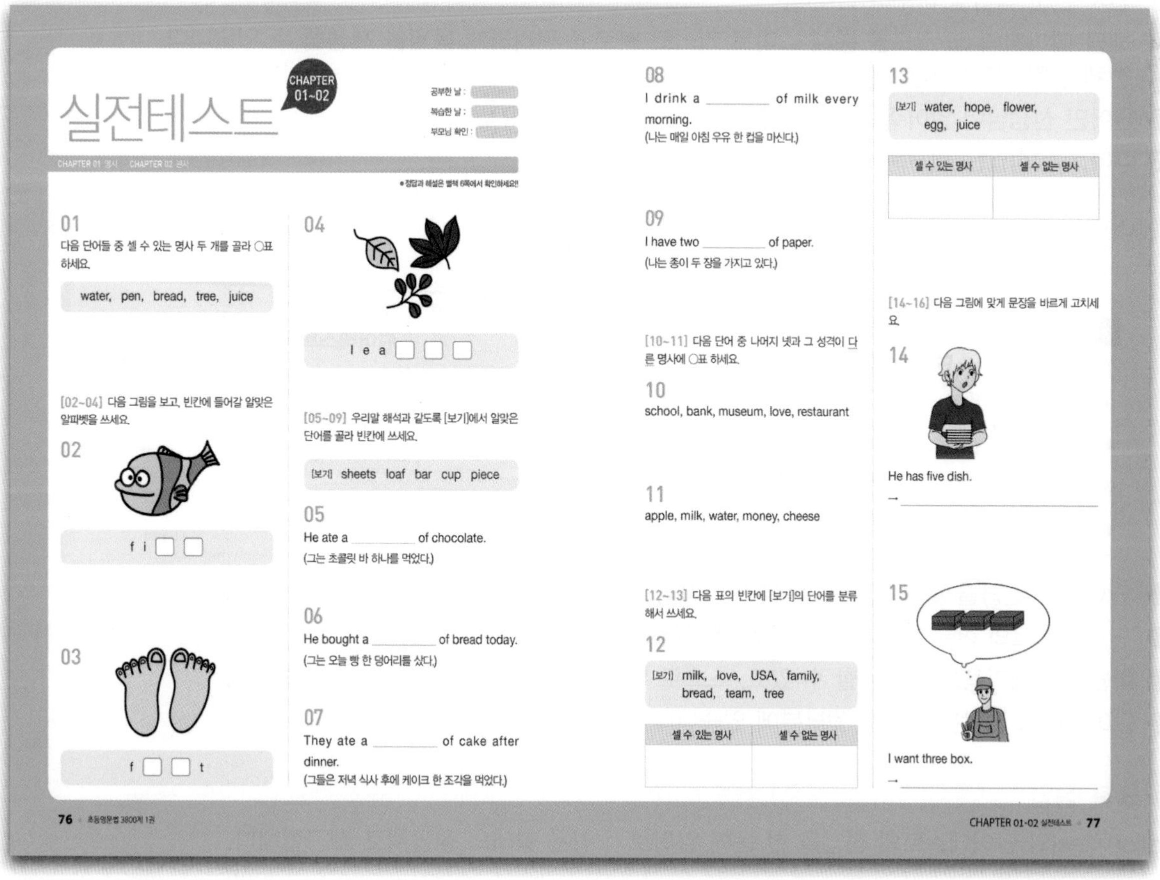
실전테스트 CHAPTER 01~02

공부한 날 : / 복습한 날 : / 부모님 확인 :

CHAPTER 01 명사 · CHAPTER 02 관사

* 정답과 해설은 별책 6쪽에서 확인하세요!

01 다음 단어들 중 셀 수 있는 명사 두 개를 골라 ○표 하세요.
water, pen, bread, tree, juice

[02~04] 다음 그림을 보고, 빈칸에 들어갈 알맞은 알파벳을 쓰세요.

02 f i □ □

03 f □ □ t

04 l e a □ □ □

[05~09] 우리말 해석과 같도록 [보기]에서 알맞은 단어를 골라 빈칸에 쓰세요.

[보기] sheets loaf bar cup piece

05 He ate a ________ of chocolate. (그는 초콜릿 바 하나를 먹었다.)

06 He bought a ________ of bread today. (그는 오늘 빵 한 덩어리를 샀다.)

07 They ate a ________ of cake after dinner. (그들은 저녁 식사 후에 케이크 한 조각을 먹었다.)

08 I drink a ________ of milk every morning. (나는 매일 아침 우유 한 컵을 마신다.)

09 I have two ________ of paper. (나는 종이 두 장을 가지고 있다.)

[10~11] 다음 단어 중 나머지 넷과 그 성격이 다른 명사에 ○표 하세요.

10 school, bank, museum, love, restaurant

11 apple, milk, water, money, cheese

[12~13] 다음 표의 빈칸에 [보기]의 단어를 분류해서 쓰세요.

12 [보기] milk, love, USA, family, bread, team, tree

셀 수 있는 명사	셀 수 없는 명사

13 [보기] water, hope, flower, egg, juice

셀 수 있는 명사	셀 수 없는 명사

[14~16] 다음 그림에 맞게 문장을 바르게 고치세요.

14 He has five dish. →

15 I want three box. →

76 초등영문법 3800제 1권 / CHAPTER 01-02 실전테스트 77

워크북 구성 및 활용법 워크북은 아래와 같은 방법으로 활용하세요.

1. 단어쓰기 연습

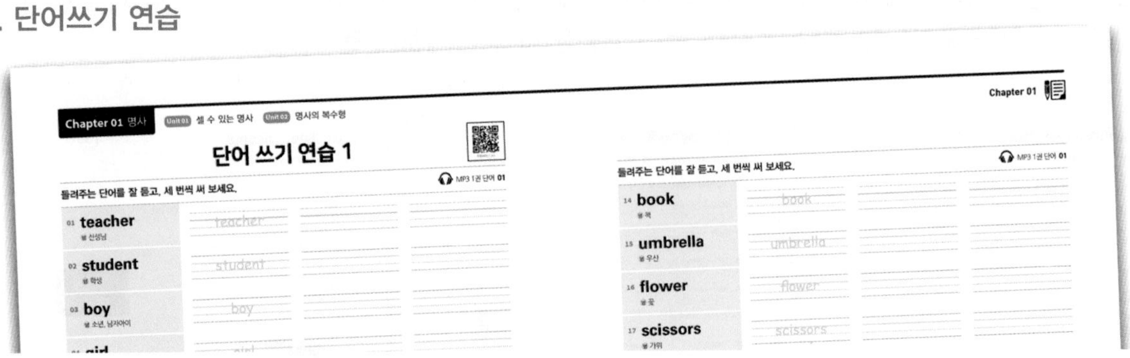

❶ 먼저 본문 학습을 마무리 합니다.

❷ 해당 페이지의 QR코드를 통해 스마트 기기로 빠르고 편리하게 음원을 재생할 수 있습니다. 전체 음원 파일은 마더텅 홈페이지(www.toptutor.co.kr)에서 다운로드 가능합니다.

❸ 원어민 선생님이 읽어주는 영단어를 잘 듣고 안내선 안에 영어 단어 철자를 세 번씩 쓰세요.

2. 받아쓰기 시험 (Dictation Test)

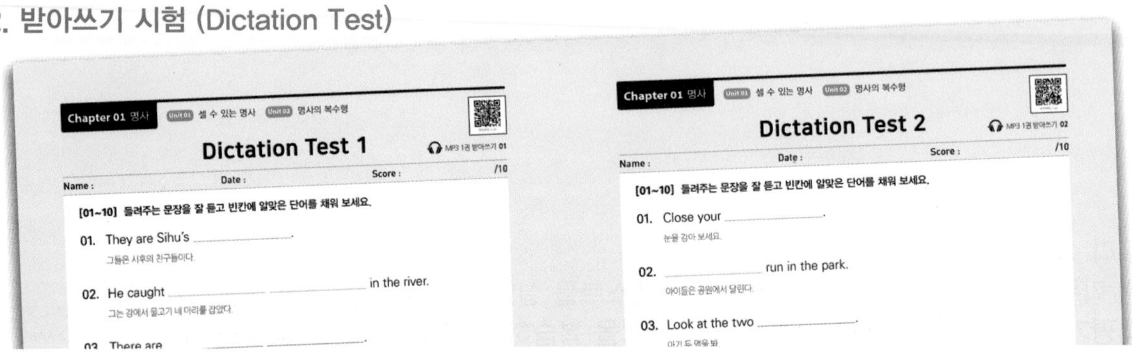

❶ 먼저 본문 학습을 마무리 합니다.

❷ 해당 페이지의 QR코드를 통해 스마트 기기로 빠르고 편리하게 음원을 재생할 수 있습니다. 전체 음원 파일은 마더텅 홈페이지(www.toptutor.co.kr)에서 다운로드 가능합니다.

❸ 원어민 선생님이 읽어주는 문장을 잘 듣고, 빈칸을 채우세요.

❹ 받아쓰기 정답은 워크북 뒷부분에 있습니다.

3. 단어테스트

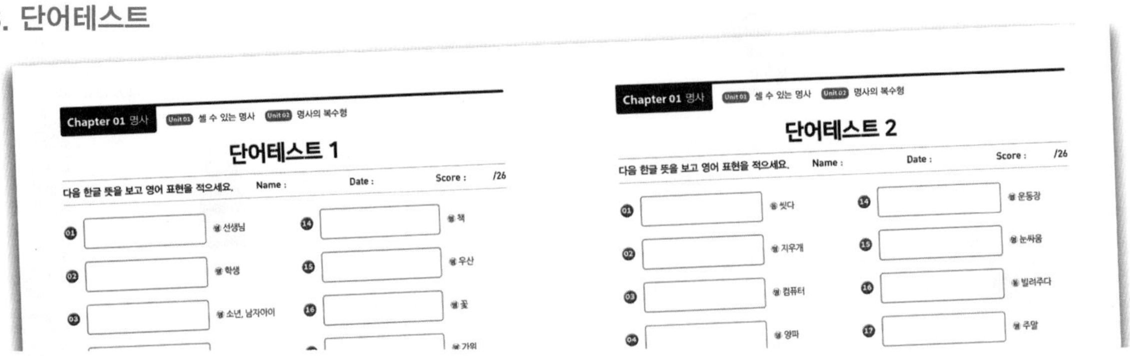

❶ 단어쓰기 연습을 하며, 단어들을 암기합니다.

❷ 단어테스트의 한글 뜻을 보고 암기한 영단어를 써 보세요.

❸ 학원에서 평가용으로 활용할 수 있고, 스스로 확인하는 용도로 활용할 수도 있습니다.

❹ 단어테스트 정답은 워크북 뒷부분에 있습니다.

4. 워크북 정답

Dictation Test와 단어테스트의 정답을 한 눈에 알아보기 쉬운 형태의 정답지로 제공합니다.

영문법 판매 1위, 중학영문법 3800제의 초등시리즈

초등영문법 3800제

1 LEVEL

입문 1단계 CONTENTS

Chapter 01 명사

이 챕터에서는 사람, 장소, 사물, 시간의 이름인 '명사'에 대해 익히고,
명사가 여러 개 있을 때는 어떻게 나타내는지 알려 줄게요.

☆ 학습 방향 및 배울 내용 미리보기 ☆

☐ **Unit 01 : a student, a school, a book, an hour**
셀 수 있는 명사
셀 수 있는 명사가 한 개 있을 때 어떻게 쓰는지 배워 봐요.

▼

☐ **Unit 02 : flowers, buses, babies, tomatoes, leaves**
명사의 복수형
셀 수 있는 명사가 여러 개일 때는 어떻게 쓰는지 배워 봐요.

▼

☐ **Unit 03 : the sun, the moon, love, hope**
셀 수 없는 명사
셀 수 없는 명사에는 무엇이 있는지 알아 봐요.

▼

☐ **Unit 04 : two cups of milk**
셀 수 없는 명사의 수량표현
셀 수 없는 명사는 복수형이 없기 때문에 단위를 나타내는 단어의 도움을 받아 수량을 나타낼 수 있어요. 셀 수 없는 명사의 수량표현을 배워 봐요.

단어 미리보기

이 챕터에 나올 단어들 중 이미 알고 있는 단어가 있나요?
맞는 뜻을 골라 체크해 봐요.

날짜 : 이름 : 알고 있는 단어의 수 : /24개

No.	아는 단어	단어	품사	알맞은 뜻에 체크 표시해 봐요.			
1	☑	student	명사	학생	☑	선생님	☐
2	☐	boy	명사	소녀	☐	소년	☐
3	☐	brother	명사	언니, 누나	☐	형, 오빠	☐
4	☐	month	명사	해(연/년)	☐	달(월)	☐
5	☐	flower	명사	풀	☐	꽃	☐
6	☐	story	명사	이야기	☐	일기	☐
7	☐	foot	명사	발가락	☐	발	☐
8	☐	eraser	명사	연필	☐	지우개	☐
9	☐	zoo	명사	박물관	☐	동물원	☐
10	☐	butterfly	명사	나비	☐	애벌레	☐
11	☐	short	형용사	긴	☐	짧은	☐
12	☐	leg	명사	팔	☐	다리	☐
13	☐	like	동사	싫어하다	☐	좋아하다	☐
14	☐	meet	동사	만나다	☐	먹다	☐
15	☐	dinner	명사	점심	☐	저녁	☐
16	☐	world	명사	단어	☐	세계	☐
17	☐	again	부사	다시	☐	항상	☐
18	☐	vegetable	명사	과일	☐	채소	☐
19	☐	dream	명사	꿈	☐	현실	☐
20	☐	help	명사	학교	☐	도움	☐
21	☐	friendship	명사	우정	☐	친구	☐
22	☐	usually	부사	가끔	☐	보통	☐
23	☐	desk	명사	책상	☐	책	☐
24	☐	chair	명사	분필	☐	의자	☐

UNIT 01 셀 수 있는 명사

a student, a school, a book, an hour

❖ POiNT 1 ❖

명사는 사람, 장소, 사물, 시간의 이름을 말해요. 명사에는 셀 수 있는 명사와 셀 수 없는 명사가 있어요.

❖ POiNT 2 ❖

a나 an은 셀 수 있는 명사의 단수와 짝꿍이에요.

명사가 하나일 때는 앞에 'a'를 붙여요.

발음이 모음(a, e, i, o, u)으로 시작하는 명사 앞에는 'an'을 써요.

a book
책 한 권

a table
탁자 한 개

an apple
사과 한 개

an egg
계란 한 알

Check and Write

A 다음 문장에서 셀 수 있는 명사를 찾아 (   ) 안에 쓰고, 문장을 다시 쓰세요.

1.

I have a brother. ⇨ (brother)

나는 남동생 한 명이 있다.

I have a brother.

2.

I have a pencil. ⇨ (   )

나는 연필 한 자루를 가지고 있다.

____

B (   ) 안에서 알맞은 표현을 찾아 동그라미하고, 완성한 문장을 다시 쓰세요.

1. There are 24 hours in (a / an) (week / day). 하루에는 24시간이 있다.

There are 24 hours in a day.

2. You need (a / an) (umbrella / pencil) when it rains. 비가 올 때 너는 우산이 필요하다.

____

C 다음 사진을 보고, 빈칸을 채워 질문에 대한 대답을 완성하세요.

1. *Q*: What is this? 이건 뭐야?

   A: It is ___a___ ___book___. 그건 책이야.

2. *Q*: What is it on the book? 그 책 위에 뭐가 있어?

   A: There is ________ ________ on the book. 책 위에 사과 한 개가 있어.

정답과 해설 p.2

UNIT **02** 명사의 복수형

flowers, buses, babies, tomatoes, leaves

❖ POiNT 1 ❖

셀 수 있는 명사가 여러 개 있을 때는 복수형으로 써요. 아래와 같은 규칙으로 복수형을 씁니다.

대부분의 셀 수 있는 명사는 -s를 붙여서 복수형을 만들어요.

flower + -s ⇨ flowers

student + -s ⇨ students

book + -s ⇨ books

orange + -s ⇨ oranges

-s, -sh, -ch, -x로 끝나면 -es를 붙여요.

bus ⇨ buses dish ⇨ dishes

church ⇨ churches

box ⇨ boxes

자음 + y로 끝나면 y를 i로 바꾸고 -es를 붙여요.

baby ⇨ babies

story ⇨ stories

lady ⇨ ladies

자음 + o로 끝나면 -es를 붙여요.

tomato ⇨ tomatoes

potato ⇨ potatoes

-f(e)로 끝나면 -f(e)를 v로 고치고 -es를 붙여요.

leaf ⇨ leaves wolf ⇨ wolves

knife ⇨ knives

항상 복수형태로 쓰는 명사 : scissors, pants, glasses

❖ POiNT 2 ❖

복수형이 불규칙하게 변하는 명사도 있어요.

단수와 복수의 형태가 같은 명사가 있다는 것에 주의해요.

man ⇨ men woman ⇨ women
foot ⇨ feet tooth ⇨ teeth
mouse ⇨ mice child ⇨ children

sheep ⇨ sheep
deer ⇨ deer
fish ⇨ fish

Check and Write

빈칸에 주어진 단어의 복수형을 써서 문장을 완성하고, 완성한 문장을 다시 쓰세요.

1. 

student There are five students.

다섯 명의 학생들이 있다.

There are five students.

2. 

dish They are washing the ________.

그들은 설거지를 하고 있다.

3. 

potato The baby has many ________.

아기는 감자를 많이 갖고 있다.

정답과 해설 p.2

Practice 1 셀 수 있는 명사의 단수형과 복수형을 익혀보아요.

다음 문장에 알맞은 단어를 보기 에서 골라 빈칸에 써 보세요. (a나 an이 필요하면 알맞은 것을 골라 같이 쓰세요.)

A On the desk

보기 pencil book scissors computer eraser

1. ___a___ ___pencil___ 연필 한 자루

2. ________ ________ 지우개 하나

3. a pair of ________ 가위 한 개

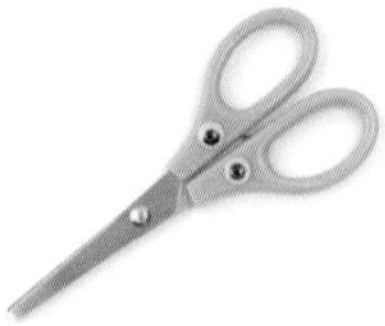

4. ________ ________ 컴퓨터 한 대

5. ________ ________ 책 한 권

B In the refrigerator

보기 onion apples bananas tomatoes egg

1. ________ ________ 계란 한 알

2. two ________ 사과 두 개

3. three ________ 바나나 세 개

4. ________ ________ 양파 한 개

5. three ________ 토마토 세 개

정답과 해설 p.2

C In the living room

보기	clock	sofa	table	flowers	cat

1. There is ______________ ______________. 탁자 한 개가 있다.

2. There are three ______________ on the table. 탁자 위에는 꽃 세 송이가 있다.

3. There is ______________ ______________.
   소파가 한 개 있다.

4. There is ______________ ______________ on the sofa.
   소파 위에 고양이 한 마리가 있다.

5. There is ______________ ______________ on the wall.
   벽에 시계 하나가 있다.

D Sihu's friends

보기	students	buses	glasses	friends	fish

1. There are 30 ______________ in Sihu's class.
   시후의 반에는 30명의 학생들이 있다.

2. Mina wears ______________. 미나는 안경을 쓴다.

3. Junwoo caught two ______________ in the river.
   준우는 강에서 물고기 두 마리를 잡았다.

4. Nayeon missed two ______________ this morning.
   나연이는 오늘 아침 버스 두 대를 놓쳤다.

5. They are Sihu's ______________.
   그들은 시후의 친구들이다.

정답과 해설 p.2

Practice 2 문장속에서 셀 수 있는 명사의 단수형과 복수형을 확실히 익혀보아요.

우리말 뜻과 같도록 (   ) 안의 명사를 알맞게 바꾸어서 다음 문장들을 완성하세요.

1. There were four (apple) in the refrigerator yesterday.
   어제 냉장고에는 사과 네 개가 있었다.
   ➔ There were four apples in the refrigerator yesterday.

2. Dad ate (apple) this morning. 아빠는 오늘 아침에 사과 한 개를 드셨다.
   ➔ ______________________________.

3. It has snowed for three (day). 3일 동안 눈이 내렸다.
   ➔ ______________________________.

4. There are many (child) on the playground for a snowball fight.
   눈싸움을 하기 위해 운동장에 많은 아이들이 있다.
   ➔ ______________________________.

5. Crunch, crunch, crunch. His (foot) sank into the snow.
   뽀드득, 뽀드득, 뽀드득. 그의 두 발이 눈 속에 빠졌다.
   ➔ Crunch, crunch, crunch.
   ______________________________.

6. It is raining now! I have two (umbrella) in the classroom!
   지금 비가 오고 있어! 나 교실에 우산 두 개 있어!
   ➔ It is raining now! ______________________________!

7. Do you want me to lend you (umbrella)? 내가 우산 한 개 빌려 줄까?
   ➔ ______________________________?

정답과 해설 p.2

8.

My (sock) are wet!

내 양말이 젖었어!

➔ ____________________

____________________!

9.

There are seven (day) in a week. 한 주에는 7일이 있다.

➔ ____________________

____________________.

10. I sleep for 10 (hour) a day on weekends. It's heaven!

나는 주말엔 하루에 10시간 동안 자. 그건 천국이야!

➔ ____. It's heaven!

11. Will you run (errand) for me, please? 나를 위해 심부름 하나 해주겠니?

➔ ____?

12. Would you put these two (box) out? 이 상자 두 개를 밖에 버려줄래?

➔ ____?

13. Can you sweep the fallen (leaf) in the yard?

마당에 있는 낙엽들을 쓸어줄래?

➔ ____

____?

14. Please tell me some fun (story). 나에게 재미있는 이야기들을 들려줘.

➔ ____.

정답과 해설 p.2

15. Brush your (tooth) after eating chocolate!
초콜릿을 먹고 나서 이를 닦아!

➔ ______________________________!

16. All (man) must choose between two (path).
모든 사람들은 두 가지 길 중에 하나를 골라야 해.

➔ ______________________________.

17.

(Fish) are (friend), not food.
물고기들은 친구들이지, 음식이 아니야.

➔ ______________________________,
not food.

18.

We all make (mistake).
우리는 모두 실수(들)를 한다.

➔ ______________________________
______________________________.

19. All (child) are born artists. 모든 아이들은 타고난 예술가이다. [피카소]

➔ ______________________________.

20. All our (dream) can come true, if we have the courage to pursue them. 우리가 그것들을 좇을 용기가 있다면, 우리의 꿈들 모두가 이루어질 것이다. [월트 디즈니]

➔ ______________________________,
if we have the courage to pursue them.

정답과 해설 p.2

Practice 3 셀 수 있는 명사의 복수형을 익혀보아요.

다음 우리말 뜻을 참고하여 ( ) 안의 명사를 단수형 또는 복수형으로 알맞게 바꾸어 문장을 다시 쓰세요.

1.

Do you see (deer)?
너는 사슴 한 마리를 보니?

➔ Do you see a deer ____________?

2.

They are (twin).
그들은 쌍둥이야.

➔ ____________ ____________.

3. I see two (wolf) at the zoo. 나는 동물원에서 늑대 두 마리를 본다.

➔ ____________.

4.

They are two (fox), not (wolf).
그것들은 여우 두 마리지, 늑대들이 아니야.

➔ ____________, ____________.

5.

Ugh! I saw three (mouse)!
으악! 나 쥐 세 마리 봤어!

➔ Ugh! ____________ ____________!

6. There are five (deer) in the forest. 숲에 사슴 다섯 마리가 있어.

➔ ____________.

정답과 해설 p.2

7. I see many (butterfly) in the countryside. 나는 시골에서 많은 나비들을 본다.

➔ ____.

8. Look at the two (baby)! 저기 아기 두 명 좀 봐!

➔ ____!

9. (Child) run in the park. 공원에서 아이들이 뛴다.

➔ ______________________________.

10. There are three (woman) in my house; my mother, my older sister and me. 우리 집에는 세 명의 여자가 있는데, 나의 엄마, 언니, 그리고 나다.

➔ ____;
my mother, my older sister and me.

11.

I have (present) for you.
너를 위한 선물 하나가 있어.

➔ ____________________
____________________.

12.

It has really short (leg)!
그것은 진짜 짧은 다리를 가졌어!

➔ ____________________
____________________!

13. There is (orange) in the refrigerator.
냉장고에 오렌지 하나가 있어.

➔ ____.

14. Close your (eye). 눈을 감아 봐.

➔ ____.

15. I don't feel my (toe). 내 발가락들이 느껴지지 않아(내 발가락들에 감각이 없어).

➔ ____.

16. I finally got (cat)! 나 결국 고양이 한 마리 생겼어!

➔ ____!

17. It peed on my (pant). 그게 내 바지 위에 오줌 쌌어.

➔ ______________________________.

18. I need a pair of (pant) and two pairs of (shoe).
저는 바지 한 벌과 신발 두 켤레가 필요해요.

➔ ____.

19. Captain America and Iron Man are my favorite (hero)!
캡틴 아메리카와 아이언 맨은 내가 가장 좋아하는 영웅들이야!

➔ ____!

20. I wear (glass). 나는 안경을 쓴다.

➔ ____.

정답과 해설 p.2

Let's Practice More!

SET 01

학습목표 1 | a와 an의 쓰임을 익혀보아요.　　공부한 날 :　　맞은 개수 : /12개

주어진 단어 앞에 a 또는 an을 붙여 문장의 빈칸에 쓰세요.

01. pencil　I don't have ___a___ ___pencil___.
나는 연필 한 자루를 가지고 있지 않다.

02. computer　Mina wants ________ ________ for her birthday.
미나는 그녀의 생일 선물로 컴퓨터 한 대를 원한다.

03. book　We read ________ ________ in the library.
우리는 도서관에서 책 한 권을 읽었다.

04. eraser　Will you lend me ________ ________?
나에게 지우개 한 개를 빌려줄래?

05. banana　The monkey is eating ________ ________.
그 원숭이는 바나나 한 개를 먹고 있다.

06. table　There is ________ ________ in the kitchen.
부엌에는 탁자 한 개가 있다.

07. tomato　Is there ________ ________ in the basket?
바구니에 토마토 한 개가 있니?

08. flower　Junsu gave me ________ ________.
준수가 나에게 꽃 한 송이를 줬다.

09. egg　You have ________ ________ for breakfast.
너는 아침 식사로 계란 한 알을 먹는다.

10. cat　Dad bought me ________ ________.
아빠가 나에게 고양이 한 마리를 사주셨다.

11. sofa　There is ________ ________ in the living room.
거실 안에는 소파 한 개가 있다.

12. clock　There is ________ ________ on the wall.
벽 위에는 시계 하나가 있다.

정답과 해설 p.3

Let's Practice More!

SET 02

학습목표 1 | a와 an의 쓰임을 익혀보아요.

공부한 날 :   맞은 개수 : /14개

주어진 단어 앞에 a 또는 an을 붙여 문장의 빈칸에 쓰세요.

01. apple — You ate ___an___ ___apple___ this morning.
너는 오늘 아침에 사과 한개를 먹었다.

02. student — She is ________ ________.
그녀는 학생이다.

03. fish — Dad caught ________ ________ in the river.
아빠가 강에서 물고기 한 마리를 잡으셨다.

04. bus — Nayeon took ________ ________ to get here.
나연이는 여기에 오기 위해 버스를 탔다.

05. errand — Will you run ________ ________ for me?
나를 위해 심부름 하나를 해주겠니?

06. wolf — There was ________ ________ at the zoo.
동물원에 늑대 한 마리가 있었다.

07. good day — We had ________ ________ ________ today.
오늘 우리는 좋은 하루를 보냈다.

08. umbrella — Did you bring ________ ________?
너는 우산을 가져왔니?

09. box — I need ________ ________ for these books.
나는 이 책들을 담을 상자 한 개가 필요해.

10. story — My grandmother told me ________ ________.
나의 할머니는 나에게 이야기 하나를 들려주셨다.

11. bad tooth — You have ________ ________ ________.
너는 충치 한 개를 가지고 있다.

12. mistake — Anyone can make ________ ________.
누구나 실수를 할 수 있다.

13. gift — I have ________ ________ for Mom.
나는 엄마를 위한 선물 한 개를 가지고 있다.

14. onion — Mom and I bought ________ ________.
엄마와 나는 양파 한 개를 샀다.

정답과 해설 p.3

Let's Practice More!

SET 03

학습목표 1 | a와 an의 쓰임을 익혀보아요. 　　공부한 날 : 　　맞은 개수 : 　/14개

주어진 단어 앞에 a 또는 an을 붙여 문장의 빈칸에 쓰세요.

01. deer　Did you see ___a___ ___deer___?
너는 사슴 한 마리를 봤니?

02. hero　Iron Man is ______ ______.
Iron Man(아이언 맨)은 영웅이다.

03. mouse　There was ______ ______ in the room.
방에 쥐 한마리가 있었다.

04. older sister　Mina has ______ ______ ______.
미나는 언니 한 명이 있다.

05. butterfly　We saw ______ ______ outside.
우리는 밖에서 나비 한 마리를 봤다.

06. woman　I met ______ ______ wearing sunglasses.
나는 선글라스를 쓴 여자 한 명을 만났다.

07. orange　There is ______ ______ in the refrigerator.
냉장고에 오렌지 한 개가 있다.

08. present　They have ______ ______ for you.
그들은 너를 위한 선물 한 개를 가지고 있다.

09. kid　Hayul is just ______ ______.
하율이는 단지 어린 아이이다.

10. baby　She knows how to hold ______ ______.
그녀는 아기를 안는 방법을 안다.

11. police officer　My father is ______ ______ ______.
나의 아버지는 경찰관이시다.

12. dream　I had ______ ______ last night.
나는 어젯밤에 꿈을 꿨다.

13. hour　The baby slept for ______ ______.
그 아기는 한 시간 동안 잠을 잤다.

14. eye　He has ______ ______ for fashion.
그는 패션에 대한 안목을 가지고 있다.

정답과 해설 p.3

Let's Practice More!

SET 04

학습목표 2 | 셀 수 있는 명사의 복수형을 만들어 보아요. 공부한 날 : 맞은 개수 : /12개

주어진 철자로 시작하는 단어를 빈칸에 넣어 문장을 완성하세요.

01. F ish ______ are friends, not food. 물고기들은 친구들이지, 음식이 아니야.

02. I saw three m__________ over there. 나 저기서 쥐 세 마리 봤어.

03. I read five b__________ this summer. 나는 이번 여름에 책 다섯 권을 읽었다.

04. There are three f__________ on the table. 탁자 위에 꽃 세 송이가 있다.

05. Mina doesn't wear g__________. 미나는 안경을 쓰지 않는다.

06. Nayeon missed two b__________. 나연이는 버스 두 대를 놓쳤다.

07. Those kids are Sihu's f__________. 저 아이들은 시후의 친구들이다.

08. I have a pair of s__________. 나는 가위 한 개가 있다.

09. There are ten s__________ in my class. 우리 반에는 열 명의 학생들이 있다.

10. It snowed for three d__________ last week. 지난주에 3일 동안 눈이 내렸다.

11. Many c__________ are on the playground. 많은 아이들이 운동장에 있다.

12. There were four a__________. 사과 네 개가 있었다.

정답과 해설 p.3

Let's Practice More!

SET 05

학습목표 2 | 셀 수 있는 명사의 복수형을 만들어 보아요. 공부한 날 : 맞은 개수 : /14개

주어진 철자로 시작하는 단어를 빈칸에 넣어 문장을 완성하세요.

01. His f<u>eet</u>________ sank into the snow. 그의 두 발이 눈 속에 빠졌다.

02. I have two u__________ in the classroom. 나는 교실에 우산 두 개가 있다.

03. Your s__________ are wet. 너의 양말이 젖었어.

04. All c__________ are born artists. 모든 아이들은 타고난 예술가이다.

05. There are seven d__________ in a week. 한 주에는 7일이 있다.

06. Sihu sleeps for ten h__________ on weekends. 시후는 주말에 10시간 동안 잔다.

07. Can you put these two b__________ out? 이 상자 두 개를 밖에 버려줄래?

08. Tell me some fun s__________. 나에게 재미있는 이야기들을 들려줘.

09. You can see fallen l__________ in fall. 너는 가을에 낙엽들을 볼 수 있다.

10. Brush your t__________ after lunch. 점심을 먹고 이를 닦아.

11. People make m__________. 사람들은 실수(들)를 한다.

12. Our d__________ can come true. 우리의 꿈들은 이루어질 수 있다.

13. They saw two w__________ at the zoo. 그들은 동물원에서 늑대 두 마리를 봤다.

14. These are f__________, not dogs. 이것들은 여우들이지, 개들이 아니야.

정답과 해설 p.3

Let's Practice More!

SET 06

학습목표 2 | 셀 수 있는 명사의 복수형을 만들어 보아요. 공부한 날 : 맞은 개수 : /14개

주어진 철자로 시작하는 단어를 빈칸에 넣어 문장을 완성하세요.

01. There are d<u>eer</u>______ in the forest. 숲에 사슴들이 있다.

02. I saw many b__________ in the mountain. 나는 산에서 많은 나비들을 봤다.

03. Those b__________ look the same. 저 아기들은 똑같아 보인다.

04. Mina and I are t__________. 미나와 나는 쌍둥이이다.

05. C__________ are running in the park. 아이들이 공원에서 달리고 있다.

06. We met three w__________ on the street. 우리는 길에서 세 명의 여자들을 만났다.

07. Do they like o__________? 그들은 오렌지들을 좋아하니?

08. Close your e__________, please. 눈을 감아주세요.

09. I don't feel my t__________. 내 발가락들이 느껴지지 않아(내 발가락들에 감각이 없어).

10. The dog has short l__________. 그 개는 짧은 다리를 가지고 있다.

11. He has many Pokémon f__________.
그는 포켓몬 피규어를 많이 가지고 있다.

12. Junsu needs two k__________. 준수는 칼 두 자루를 필요로 한다.

13. Nayeon has three c__________. 나연이는 고양이 세 마리가 있다.

14. My parents are my h__________. 내 부모님은 나의 영웅이다.

정답과 해설 p.3

Let's Practice More!

SET 07

학습목표 3 | 셀 수 있는 명사를 사용해 문장을 만들어 보세요. 공부한 날 : 맞은 개수 : /20개

우리말 뜻에 알맞게 빈칸을 채워 문장을 완성하세요.

01.

I wear __glasses__.

나는 안경을 쓴다.

02.

__________ __________ is eating a __________.

원숭이 한 마리가 바나나를 먹고 있다.

03. He is __________ __________. 그는 영웅이다.

04. The __________ are __________. 그 아기들은 쌍둥이다.

05.

We can see fallen __________ in fall.

우리는 가을에 낙엽을 볼 수 있다.

06.

Nayeon has __________ __________.

나연이는 세 마리의 고양이가 있다.

07. Did you see __________ in the forest?

너는 숲에서 사슴들을 봤니?

08. Nayeon has __________ __________. 나연이에게는 연필이 한 자루 있다.

정답과 해설 p.3

09. Do you have ______________? 너는 가위가 있니?

10. Mom is cutting ______________ ______________. 엄마는 양파 한 개를 썰고 계신다.

11. There are ______________ ______________ in the shop.
그 가게에는 꽃들이 많다.

12. There are ______________ ______________ in the park. 공원에 다섯 명의 학생들이 있다.

13. Hayul is just ______________ ______________. 하율이는 단지 어린 아이이다.

14. I am ______________ ______________ of Sihu. 나는 시후의 친구이다.

15. My brother sleeps for ______________ ______________. 내 남동생은 여덟 시간 동안 잔다.

16. My ______________ sank into the snow. 나의 두 발이 눈 속에 빠졌다.

17. She has ______________ ______________ in her bag.
그녀는 가방 안에 우산 한 개가 있다.

18. There are seven ______________ in ______________ week. 한 주에는 7일이 있다.

19. Junsu ate ______________ ______________ today. 준수는 오늘 두 마리의 생선을 먹었다.

20. Tell me your ______________.
나에게 너의 이야기들을 들려줘.

정답과 해설 p.3

Let's Practice More!

SET 08

학습목표 3 | **셀 수 있는 명사를 사용해 문장을 만들어 보세요.** 공부한 날 : 맞은 개수 : /20개

우리말 뜻에 알맞게 빈칸을 채워 문장을 완성하세요.

01. 

Close your ___eyes___, please.
눈을 감아주세요.

02. 

Many __________ are running on the playground.
많은 아이들이 운동장에서 달리고 있다.

03. There are __________ __________ on the table.
탁자 위에 오렌지 두 개가 있다.

04. We saw many __________ outside. 우리는 밖에서 많은 나비들을 봤다.

05. She doesn't feel her __________.
그녀는 그녀의 발가락들이 느껴지지 않는다(그녀의 발가락들에 감각이 없다).

06. Mina had __________ __________ for lunch. 미나는 점심으로 사과 두 개를 먹었다.

07. Will you lend me __________ __________? 나에게 지우개 하나를 빌려줄래?

08. Brush your __________ right now. 지금 당장 너의 이를 닦아라.

09. We all make __________. 우리는 모두 실수(들)를 한다.

정답과 해설 p.3

10. Our ______________ can come true. 우리의 꿈들은 이루어질 수 있다.

11. I saw ______________ ______________ at the zoo. 나는 동물원에서 늑대 두 마리를 봤다.

12. ______________ ______________ are in the hole. 쥐 세 마리가 그 구멍 안에 있다.

13. There are 24 ______________ in ______________ day. 하루에는 24시간이 있다.

14. I have ______________ ______________ for Mom. 나는 엄마를 위한 선물 한 개를 가지고 있다.

15.

I need __________ __________ for my __________.

나는 내 고양이들을 위한 상자 한 개가 필요하다.

16.

The rabbit has __________ __________.

그 토끼는 짧은 다리를 가지고 있다.

17. Sihu needs ______________ ______________. 시후는 연필 세 자루를 필요로 한다.

18. There is ______________ ______________ in the living room. 거실에 소파 한 개가 있다.

19. They have ______________ ______________. 그들은 개 네 마리를 가지고 있다.

20. Please run ______________ ______________ for me. 나를 위해 심부름 하나만 해 줘.

정답과 해설 p.3

UNIT

03 the sun, the moon, love, hope

셀 수 없는 명사

❖ POiNT 1 ❖

셀 수 없는 명사는 일정한 형태가 없는 것을 가리켜요.

알맹이가 작은 물이나 모래도, 자르면 수가 늘어나는 치즈나 빵도, 눈에 보이지 않는 감정이나 생각, 과목, 운동, 게임을 나타내는 명사도 셀 수 없는 명사예요.

water 물

bread 빵

일정한 형태가 없는 것
물(water), 주스(juice),
빵(bread), 치즈(cheese)

soccer 축구

English 영어

운동, 과목
축구(soccer), 야구(baseball),
수학(math), 영어(English)

love 사랑

moon 달

눈에 보이지 않는 것,
세상에 단 하나뿐인 것
사랑(love), 희망(hope),
해(sun), 달(moon)

❖ POiNT 2 ❖

고유명사는 특정한 사람이나 사물의 이름을 말하는데, 마찬가지로 셀 수 없는 명사예요.
고유명사의 첫 글자는 대문자로 써요.

사람 이름	Mike(마이크)	Lucy(루시)	Nayeon(나연)	Junwoo(준우)
나라 이름	Korea(한국)	America(미국)	China(중국)	Japan(일본)
도시 이름	Busan(부산)	Seoul(서울)	London(런던)	Paris(파리)
월/요일 이름	Monday(월요일)	Tuesday(화요일)	January(1월)	February(2월)

Check and Write

A 다음 명사 중에서 셀 수 없는 명사를 찾아 [ ] 안에 쓰세요.

apple 사과

egg 계란

rice 쌀

paper 종이

banana 바나나

water 물

rice		

B 다음 셀 수 없는 명사 중에서 고유명사를 찾아 동그라미하세요.

soccer 축구

math 수학

Sihu 시후

oil 기름

hope 희망

Busan 부산

London 런던

bread 빵

December 12월

cheese 치즈

Korea 한국

juice 주스

정답과 해설 p.3

셀 수 없는 명사의 수량표현

UNIT 04 two cups of milk

❖ POiNT 1 ❖

셀 수 없는 명사는 항상 단수의 형태로 써요! a/an을 붙이지 않고, 복수형도 없어요.

a water (x)
waters (x)
⇨ **water** (o)

a milk (x)
milks (x)
⇨ **milk** (o)

a money (x)
moneys (x)
⇨ **money** (o)

❖ POiNT 2 ❖

셀 수 없는 명사는 a/an을 붙이지 않고 복수형을 쓸 수 없지만 단위를 나타내는 단어의 도움으로 수량을 나타낼 수 있어요.

- a cup of milk 우유 한 컵 — two cups of milk 우유 두 컵
- a glass of water 물 한 잔 — three glasses of water 물 세 잔
- a bar of chocolate 초콜릿 바 한 개 — two bars of chocolate 초콜릿 바 두 개
- a bar of soap 비누 한 개 — two bars of soap 비누 두 개
- a bottle of juice 주스 한 병 — four bottles of juice 주스 네 병
- a sheet of paper 종이 한 장 — four sheets of paper 종이 네 장
- a loaf of bread 빵 한 덩어리 — two loaves of bread 빵 두 덩어리
- a slice of cheese 치즈 한 장 — three slices of cheese 치즈 세 장
- a piece of pizza 피자 한 조각 — two pieces of pizza 피자 두 조각
- a piece of furniture 가구 한 점 — five pieces of furniture 가구 다섯 점

⇨ 단위를 나타내는 명사를 복수형으로 고쳐준다는 사실 잊지 마세요!

Check and Write

주어진 그림에 맞는 수량 표현을 보기에서 찾아 [   ] 에 써 보세요.

보기

a piece of	two glasses of	two loaves of
two slices of	a cup of	a bar of

[two loaves of] bread

빵 두 덩어리

[   ] juice

주스 두 잔

[   ] cheese

치즈 두 장

[   ] milk

우유 한 컵

[   ] chocolate

초콜릿 바 한 개

[   ] pizza

피자 한 조각

정답과 해설 p.3

Practice 1 셀 수 있는 명사와 셀 수 없는 명사를 구분해 보아요.

다음 문장에 알맞은 단어를 보기 에서 골라 빈칸에 써 보세요.

A Love, love, love

보기 math Love Monday Sihu America English

1. Mina is from ___America___. 미나는 미국에서 왔다.

2. She likes ________. 그녀는 영어를 좋아한다.

3. She doesn't like ________. 그녀는 수학을 좋아하지 않는다.

4. She loves ________, because she can meet ________ then.
그녀는 월요일을 좋아하는데 왜냐하면 그녀가 그 때 시후를 만날 수 있기 때문이다.

5. ________ is great. 사랑은 위대해.

B I'm thirsty!

보기 water soccer juice glasses water

1. I played ________ on the playground. 나는 운동장에서 축구를 했다.

2. I was thirsty. I needed some ________.
나는 목이 말랐다. 나는 물이 좀 필요했다.

3. I went home to drink a glass of ________.
나는 물 한 잔을 마시기 위해 집으로 갔다.

4. But there was only ________ in the refrigerator.
하지만 냉장고에는 주스만 있었다.

5. I drank two ________ of juice. 나는 주스 두 잔을 마셨다.

정답과 해설 p.3

C I'm full!

보기	pig	bread	chocolate	pizza	apple

1. An ______________ is in the basket. 바구니에 사과 한 개가 있다.

2. Two loaves of ______________ are on the table. 탁자에 빵 두 덩어리가 있다.

3. Two bars of ______________ are in my brother's room.
우리 오빠 방에 초콜릿 바 두 개가 있다.

4. I ate all of them! Then I ate three pieces of ______________ for dinner. 나는 다 먹었다! 그러고 나서 나는 저녁으로 피자 세 조각도 먹었다.

5. I'm a ______________! 난 돼지야!

D Junwoo's room

보기	paper	furniture	money	work	pants

1. There are five pieces of ______________ in my room. 내 방에는 가구 다섯 점이 있다.

2. There are my ______________ on the chair. 의자 위에 내 바지가 있다.

3. There is some ______________ in the pocket of my pants.
내 바지 주머니에는 약간의 돈이 있다.

4. There are ten sheets of ______________ on the desk.
책상 위에는 종이 열 장이 있다.

5. He has a lot of ______________ to do. 그는 할 일이 많아.

정답과 해설 p.3

Practice 2 셀 수 있는 명사와 셀 수 없는 명사를 써서 문장을 완성해 보아요.

다음 우리말 뜻과 같도록 ( )안의 단어를 순서에 맞게 배열하여 문장을 완성하세요.

1.

(blue eyes, have, I).

나는 푸른색 눈을 가지고 있다.

➜ I have blue eyes

______________.

2.

(My birthday, in March, is).

내 생일은 3월이야.

➜ ______________

______________.

3. *A*: (in February, is, My birthday). I'm older than you.

내 생일은 2월이야. 내가 너보다 나이가 많아.

B: No way! 말도 안 돼!

➜ *A*: ______________. I'm older than you.

B: No way!

4. (best, like, Saturday, I). 나는 토요일을 가장 좋아해.

➜ ______________.

5. They (basketball, play, on Saturday).

그들은 토요일에 농구를 해.

➜ They ______________.

6. I don't have any (student government, interest, in).

나는 학생회에는 어떤 관심도 없어.

➜ I don't have any ______________.

정답과 해설 p.3

7. I make lunch (with, on Sunday, mom). 나는 일요일에 엄마와 점심을 만들어.
➔ I make lunch ______________________________.

8. All men by nature (knowledge, desire). (*by nature: 태어나면서, 선천적으로)
모든 인간은 태어나면서 지식을 갈망한다. [아리스토텔레스]
➔ All men by nature ______________________________.

9. (We, a lot of, sugar, need), too. 우리는 많은 설탕도 필요해.
➔ ______________________________, too.

10. (Look, the smoke, at) in the kitchen. 부엌에 연기 좀 봐.
➔ ______________________________ in the kitchen.

11. (burned, Your mom, the food) again! 너의 엄마가 음식을 또 태웠구나!
➔ ______________________________ again!

12. Mom, you should put (in, more oil, the pan). 엄마, 팬에 더 많은 기름을 넣어야 해요.
➔ Mom, you should put ______________________________.

13. *A*: My younger brother (water, your smartphone, on, spilled)! (*spill: 엎지르다)
내 남동생이 네 스마트폰에 물을 엎질렀어!
B: It's OK. It's waterproof. 괜찮아. 그거 방수 돼.
➔ *A*: My younger brother ______________________________!
B: It's OK. It's waterproof.

14. Ugh... (water, It is not). It's pee! 으... 그거 물 아니야. 오줌이야!
➔ Ugh... ______________________________. It's pee!

정답과 해설 p.3

15.

I usually (listen to, on Sunday, music).
나는 보통 일요일에 음악을 들어.

→ I usually ______________ ______________________.

16.

We use cheese, (milk, flour, and).
우리는 치즈, 밀가루, 그리고 우유를 사용해.

→ We use cheese, ______________________.

17.

(play, They, soccer) every weekend.
그들은 주말마다 축구를 해.

→ ______________________ every weekend.

18.

(is, the sum, Success) of small efforts.
성공은 작은 노력들의 총합이다.

→ ______________________ of small efforts.

19. (not, Money, everything, is). I know because I have money and everything. 돈이 전부인 것은 아니야. 나는 돈과 모든 것을 가지고 있기 때문에 알아.

→ ______________________________________. I know because I have money and everything.

20. (I, much fear, sense) in you. 너에게서 많은 공포심이 느껴져.

→ ______________________________________ in you.

정답과 해설 p.3

Practice 3 셀 수 없는 명사를 써서 완전한 문장을 써 보아요.

다음 우리말 뜻을 참고하여 빈칸에 적절한 단어를 쓰고 문장을 다시 써 보세요.

1. 

We need __rice__ and vegetables to make fried rice.
우리는 볶음밥을 만들기 위해 쌀과 야채가 필요해.
→ We need rice and vegetables to make fried rice.

2. 

Three bottles of ________ are on the table.
세 병의 주스가 탁자 위에 있어.
→ ________________________.

3. ________ comes from plants. 빵은 식물들에서 유래한다.
→ ________________________.

4. ________ comes from animals. 우유는 동물들에서 유래한다.
→ ________________________.

5. ________ comes from animals. 고기는 동물들에서 유래한다.
→ ________________________.

6. We had ________ in April this year. 올해에는 4월에 눈이 왔었다.
→ ________________________.

7. Let's make some ________ for the baby! 아기를 위해 그늘을 만들자!
→ ________________________!

정답과 해설 p.3

8. The ______________ rises in the east.

태양은 동쪽에서 뜬다.

➔ ____.

9. "Romeo and Juliet" is a story about ______________ .

'로미오와 줄리엣'은 사랑에 대한 이야기야.

➔ ____.

10. I have a lot of ______________ to do. 나는 해야 할 숙제가 많아.

➔ ____.

11. Good friends will give you ______________ in bad situations.

좋은 친구는 나쁜 상황에서 너에게 도움을 줄 것이다.

➔ ____.

12. The English test is tomorrow, but there is still __________. I can cram!

영어 시험이 내일이지만 아직 희망이 있어. 난 벼락치기 할 수 있거든! **(*cram: 벼락치기를 하다)**

➔ The English test is tomorrow,

____. I can cram!

13. That is totally new ______________! 그것은 완전히 새로운 정보구나!

➔ ____!

14. Wasn't there just a sheet of ______________? 그저 종이 한 장만 있지 않았어?

➔ ____?

정답과 해설 p.4

15. Drinking much soft drink is not good for your ______________.

탄산음료를 많이 마시는 것은 너의 건강에 좋지 않아.

➔ ____

____.

16. We should recycle ______________ to save the environment.

우리는 환경을 구하기 위해 플라스틱을 재활용해야 해.

➔ ____

____.

17. ______________ is important to me.

우정은 나에게 중요해.

➔ ____.

18.

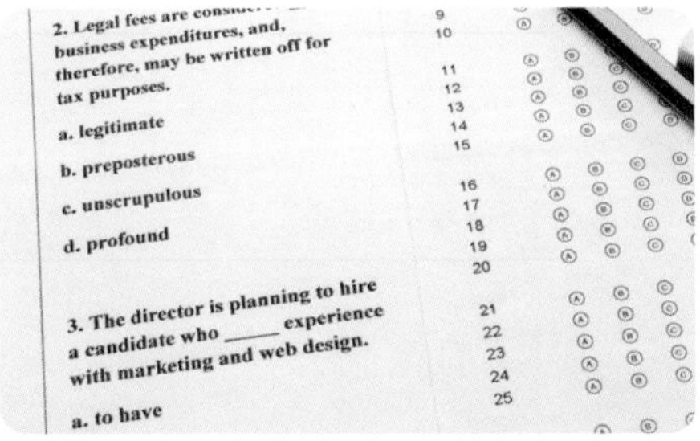

The test was made up of two __________ of paper.

시험은 종이 두 장으로 이루어져 있었어.

➔ ______________________

______________________.

19.

I eat two __________ of bread and drink a __________ of milk for breakfast.

나는 아침식사로 빵 두 덩어리와 우유 한 컵을 마셔.

➔ ______________________

____

______________________.

정답과 해설 p.4

Let's Practice More!

SET 01

학습목표 1 | 셀 수 있는 명사와 셀 수 없는 명사를 구별할 수 있어요.　　공부한 날 :　　맞은 개수 :　　/12개

다음 문장에서 셀 수 없는 명사를 모두 찾아 쓰세요.

01. We play soccer on the playground. → soccer
우리는 운동장에서 축구를 한다.

02. People think love is great. → ______
사람들은 사랑이 위대하다고 생각한다.

03. There are three bottles of juice in the fridge. → ______
냉장고 안에 주스 세 병이 있다.

04. She likes English and math. → ______
그녀는 영어와 수학을 좋아한다.

05. There are two loaves of bread on the table. → ______
탁자 위에 빵 두 덩어리가 있다.

06. Dad has a lot of work. → ______
아빠는 할 일이 많으시다.

07. You have blue eyes and blond hair. → ______
너는 푸른색 눈과 금발을 가졌다.

08. Children go to school on Monday. → ______
아이들은 월요일에 학교에 간다.

09. My birthday is in April. → ______
내 생일은 4월이야.

10. They bought some cheese and flour. → ______
그들은 약간의 치즈와 밀가루를 샀다.

11. I have some money. → ______
나는 약간의 돈을 가지고 있다.

12. Success is the sum of small efforts. → ______
성공은 작은 노력들의 합이다.

정답과 해설 p.4

Let's Practice More!

SET 02

학습목표 1 | 셀 수 있는 명사와 셀 수 없는 명사를 구별할 수 있어요. 공부한 날 : 맞은 개수 : /14개

다음 문장에서 셀 수 없는 명사를 모두 찾아 쓰세요.

01. Mom burned the food again. → food
엄마가 음식을 또 태우셨다.

02. Mina is from America. → ________
미나는 미국에서 왔다.

03. I put too much oil in the pan. → ________
나는 팬에 기름을 너무 많이 넣었다.

04. Junwoo woke up late on Saturday. → ________
준우는 토요일에 늦게 일어났다.

05. My brother spilled milk on the floor. → ________
내 남동생이 바닥에 우유를 엎질렀다.

06. Money is not everything. → ________
돈이 전부인 것은 아니다.

07. We have sugar and salt. → ________
우리는 설탕과 소금을 가지고 있다.

08. There is some furniture in the room. → ________
방에는 약간의 가구들이 있다.

09. I have no interest in studying. → ________
나는 공부에는 관심이 없다.

10. Friendship is important to me. → ________
우정은 나에게 중요하다.

11. The sun rises in the east. → ________
해는 동쪽에서 뜬다.

12. His feet sank into the snow. → ________
그의 두 발이 눈 속에 빠졌다.

13. Have the courage to pursue your dream. → ________
너의 꿈을 좇을 용기를 가져라.

14. We have a lot of homework to do today. → ________
우리는 오늘 해야 할 숙제가 많다.

정답과 해설 p.4

Let's Practice More!

SET 03

학습목표 1 | 셀 수 있는 명사와 셀 수 없는 명사를 구별할 수 있어요. 공부한 날 : 맞은 개수 : /14개

다음 문장에서 셀 수 없는 명사를 모두 찾아 쓰세요.

01. I like listening to music. → music
나는 음악 듣는 것을 좋아한다.

02. Sunshine will melt the snowman. → ______
햇빛이 그 눈사람을 녹일 것이다.

03. Have some confidence. → ______
자신감을 가져라.

04. Ten sheets of paper are on the desk. → ______
종이 열 장이 책상 위에 있다.

05. Let me give you a piece of advice. → ______
내가 너에게 조언 하나 해줄게.

06. That is totally new information! → ______
그것은 완전히 새로운 정보구나!

07. There is hope of success. → ______
성공의 희망이 있다.

08. Exercising is good for your health. → ______
운동하는 것은 너의 건강에 좋다.

09. Look at the smoke in the kitchen. → ______
부엌에 연기 좀 봐.

10. I eat a loaf of bread and drink a cup of milk. → ______
나는 빵 한 덩어리를 먹고, 우유 한 컵을 마신다.

11. Meat comes from animals. → ______
고기는 동물에서 온다(유래한다).

12. My birthday is in February. → ______
나의 생일은 2월이다.

13. Please leave me in peace. → ______
저를 조용히 내버려 두세요.

14. The test was made up of a sheet of paper. → ______
그 시험은 종이 한 장으로 이루어져 있었다.

정답과 해설 p.4

Let's Practice More!

SET 04

학습목표 2 | 단위를 사용해 명사의 수량을 표현할 수 있어요. 공부한 날 : 맞은 개수 : /12개

빈칸에 주어진 철자로 시작하는 단어를 넣어 문장을 완성하세요.

01. Mom drinks a c<u>up</u>______ of coffee. 엄마는 커피 한 잔을 드신다.

02. I eat a l__________ of bread for breakfast. 나는 아침으로 빵 한 덩어리를 먹는다.

03. Junsu wants a g__________ of Coke. 준수는 콜라 한 잔을 원한다.

04. You have two s__________ of paper. 너는 종이 두 장을 가지고 있다.

05. He drank two g__________ of water. 그는 물 두 잔을 마셨다.

06. I ordered a p__________ of cake. 나는 케이크 한 조각을 주문했다.

07. We bought three b__________ of juice. 우리는 주스 세 병을 샀다.

08. I want a p__________ of pizza. 나는 피자 한 조각을 원한다.

09. Nayeon had two s__________ of cheese. 나연이는 치즈 두 조각을 먹었다.

10. Dad wants a b__________ of wine. 아빠는 와인 한 병을 원하신다.

11. There are two b__________ of chocolate. 초콜릿 바 두 개가 있다.

12. Pass me two l__________ of bread, please. 저에게 빵 두 덩어리를 건네주세요.

정답과 해설 p.4

Let's Practice More!

SET 05

학습목표 2 | 단위를 사용해 명사의 수량을 표현할 수 있어요.　　공부한 날 :　　맞은 개수 :　　/14개

빈칸에 주어진 철자로 시작하는 단어를 넣어 문장을 완성하세요.

01. We bought a b<u>ottle</u>____ of oil. 우리는 기름 한 병을 샀다.

02. Give me a c__________ of tea, please. 저에게 차 한 잔 주세요.

03. Sihu needs a b__________ of soap. 시후는 비누 한 개가 필요하다.

04. Mark drank a g__________ of wine at my party. Mark는 내 파티에서 와인 한 잔을 마셨다.

05. There were five l__________ of bread. 빵 다섯 덩어리가 있었다.

06. I need four s__________ of paper. 나는 종이 네 장이 필요하다.

07. My brother ate three p__________ of cheese. 내 남동생은 치즈 세 조각을 먹었다.

08. You buy two b__________ of chocolate. 너는 초콜릿 바 두 개를 산다.

09. Will you give me a s__________ of paper? 나에게 종이 한 장 줄래?

10. Mom baked a l__________ of bread. 엄마는 빵 한 덩어리를 구우셨다.

11. There are two b__________ of juice on the table. 탁자 위에 주스 두 병이 있다.

12. I can eat two p__________ of cake. 나는 케이크 두 조각을 먹을 수 있다.

13. Mina wants two g__________ of juice. 미나는 주스 두 잔을 원한다.

14. He drinks two c__________ of coffee every day. 그는 매일 커피 두 잔을 마신다.

정답과 해설 p.4

Let's Practice More!

SET 06

학습목표 2 | 단위를 사용해 명사의 수량을 표현할 수 있어요. 공부한 날 : 맞은 개수 : /14개

빈칸에 주어진 철자로 시작하는 단어를 넣어 문장을 완성하세요.

01. I want three l<u>oaves</u>_____ of bread. 나는 빵 세 덩어리를 원한다.

02. Sihu drank three g__________ of water. 시후는 물 세 잔을 마셨다.

03. They bought four b__________ of juice. 그들은 주스 네 병을 샀다.

04. She ate a b__________ of chocolate. 그녀는 초콜릿 바 한 개를 먹었다.

05. Drink two c__________ of milk at night. 밤에 우유 두 컵을 마셔라.

06. There are ten s__________ of paper. 종이 열 장이 있다.

07. Mom drank two g__________ of wine. 엄마는 와인 두 잔을 드셨다.

08. We need two b__________ of oil. 우리는 기름 두 병이 필요하다.

09. I ate three p__________ of pizza for dinner. 나는 저녁으로 피자 세 조각을 먹었다.

10. Give me a p__________ of cake, please. 저에게 케이크 한 조각을 주세요.

11. I ate a l__________ of bread for breakfast. 나는 아침으로 빵 한 덩어리를 먹었다.

12. He drinks a g__________ of milk every morning. 그는 아침마다 우유 한 잔을 마신다.

13. I had two p__________ of cake for dessert. 나는 디저트로 케이크 두 조각을 먹었다.

14. I drink a c__________ of water after lunch. 나는 점심식사 후에 물 한 컵을 마신다.

정답과 해설 p.4

Let's Practice More!

SET 07

학습목표 3 | 셀 수 없는 명사를 사용해 문장을 만들어 보세요.   공부한 날 :   맞은 개수 :   /20개

다음 빈칸을 채워 우리말 뜻에 맞는 문장을 완성하세요.

01. 

We have a lot of homework to do.

우리는 해야 할 숙제가 많이 있다.

02. I ate two ______________ of ______________ for dinner. 나는 저녁으로 피자 두 조각을 먹었다.

03. 

______________ is important to me.

우정은 나에게 중요하다.

04. She drinks a ______________ of ______________.

그녀는 물 한 잔을 마신다.

05. 

______________ is not everything.

돈이 전부인 것은 아니야.

06. There is a ______________ of ______________.

치즈 한 조각이 있다.

정답과 해설 p.4

07. There is some ______________ in the pocket. 주머니에 돈이 약간 있다.

08. Please bring me three ______________ of ______________.
저에게 주스 세 병을 가져다 주세요.

09. I drink a ______________ of ______________ every morning.
나는 아침마다 우유 한 잔을 마신다.

10. He has a lot of ______________ to do. 그는 할 일이 많이 있다.

11. There were two ______________ of ______________.
초콜릿 바 두 개가 있었다.

12. It is totally new ______________. 그것은 완전히 새로운 정보이다.

13. We use ______________ and ______________. 우리는 밀가루와 우유를 사용한다.

14. Junwoo's birthday is in ______________. 준우의 생일은 3월이다.

15. There was a ______________ of ______________ in the fridge.
냉장고에 주스 한 병이 있었다.

16. I need ten ______________ of ______________. 나는 종이 열 장이 필요하다.

17. He spilled ______________ on my smartphone. 그는 내 스마트폰에 물을 엎질렀다.

18. Dad bought three ______________ of ______________. 아빠는 빵 세 덩어리를 사셨다.

19. Nayeon likes ______________ and ______________. 나연이는 영어와 수학을 좋아한다.

20. I drank two ______________ of ______________.
나는 주스 두 잔을 마셨다.

정답과 해설 p.4

Let's Practice More!

SET 08

학습목표 3 | 셀 수 없는 명사를 사용해 문장을 만들어 보세요.　　공부한 날 :　　맞은 개수 :　　/20개

다음 빈칸을 채워 우리말 뜻에 맞는 문장을 완성하세요.

01. 

There are two ___loaves___ of ___bread___.
빵 두 덩어리가 있다.

02. Mom drinks a ______________ of ______________ every day. 엄마는 매일 커피 한 잔을 드신다.

03. 

We bought a ______________ of ______________.
우리는 기름 한 병을 샀다.

04. I need ten ______________ of ______________.
나는 종이 열 장이 필요하다.

05. 

We ordered two ______________ of ______________.
우리는 케이크 두 조각을 주문했다.

06. Junsu doesn't like ______________.
준수는 수학을 좋아하지 않는다.

정답과 해설 p.4

07. I had a ______________ of ______________ for dessert.
나는 디저트로 치즈 한 조각을 먹었다.

08. You put too much ______________ in the pan. 너는 팬에 기름을 너무 많이 넣었다.

09. Please bring me a ______________ of ______________.
저에게 초콜릿 바 한 개를 가져다 주세요.

10. I ordered 10 ______________ of ______________ for the party.
나는 그 파티를 위해 와인 10병을 주문했다.

11. We bought two ______________ of ______________.
우리는 비누 두 개를 샀다.

12. Dad wants a ______________ of ______________. 아빠는 와인 한 잔을 원하신다.

13. People think ______________ is great. 사람들은 사랑이 위대하다고 생각한다.

14. I eat a ______________ of ______________ for breakfast.
나는 아침으로 빵 한 덩어리를 먹는다.

15. Mina's ______________ is in July. 미나의 생일은 7월이다.

16. I have no ______________ in studying. 나는 공부에는 관심이 없다.

17. We need much ______________. 우리는 설탕이 많이 필요하다.

18. They have three ______________ of ______________. 그들은 세 조각의 치즈를 가지고 있다.

19. Exercising is good for your ______________. 운동하는 것은 너의 건강에 좋아.

20. She ate two ______________ of ______________. 그녀는 초콜릿 바 두 개를 먹었다.

정답과 해설 p.4

Chapter 02 관사

이 챕터에서는 명사 앞에 붙는 명사의 짝꿍인 '관사'에 대해 익히고,
관사의 종류와 그것들의 차이점에 대해 배워 봐요.

☆ 학습 방향 및 배울 내용 미리보기 ☆

☐ **Unit 01 : We buy a book for Mina.**

부정관사

부정관사 a와 an이 언제 쓰이는지 알려줄게요.

▼

☐ **Unit 02 : The bike is old.**

정관사

정관사가 무엇인지, 그리고 언제 쓰이는지 알려줄게요.

단어 미리보기

이 챕터에 나올 단어들 중 이미 알고 있는 단어가 있나요?
맞는 뜻을 골라 체크해 봐요.

날짜 :　　　이름 :　　　알고 있는 단어의 수 :　　　/24개

No.	아는 단어	단어	품사	알맞은 뜻에 체크 표시해 봐요.			
1	☑	give	동사	주다	☑	받다	☐
2	☐	together	부사	따로	☐	함께	☐
3	☐	delicious	형용사	아주 맛있는	☐	맛없는	☐
4	☐	see	동사	보다	☐	듣다	☐
5	☐	cute	형용사	귀여운	☐	못생긴	☐
6	☐	shy	형용사	수줍어하는	☐	활발한	☐
7	☐	present	명사	발표	☐	선물	☐
8	☐	night	명사	밤	☐	아침	☐
9	☐	sky	명사	바다	☐	하늘	☐
10	☐	beautiful	형용사	아름다운	☐	굉장한	☐
11	☐	left	형용사	오른쪽의	☐	왼쪽의	☐
12	☐	speak	동사	말하다	☐	보다	☐
13	☐	heart	명사	마음	☐	목	☐
14	☐	doctor	명사	간호사	☐	의사	☐
15	☐	joke	명사	농담	☐	실수	☐
16	☐	bike	명사	자전거	☐	자동차	☐
17	☐	early	부사	늦게	☐	일찍	☐
18	☐	ground	명사	땅바닥	☐	천장	☐
19	☐	treasure	명사	선물	☐	보물	☐
20	☐	pet	명사	야생동물	☐	애완동물	☐
21	☐	glasses	명사	안경	☐	유리	☐
22	☐	fight	동사	싸우다	☐	화해하다	☐
23	☐	want	동사	버리다	☐	원하다	☐
24	☐	live	동사	살다	☐	죽다	☐

부정관사

UNIT 01 We buy a book for Mina.

❖ POiNT 1 ❖

명사는 항상 함께 쓰이는 짝꿍이 있어요. 바로 '관사'예요.

부정관사 a(an)의 '부정'이라는 말은 '정해지지 않았다'라는 말이에요.

즉, 부정관사는 '정해지지 않은 사람 또는 사물 하나'를 표현할 때 쓴답니다.
해석하지 않는 경우가 많고, 셀 수 있는 단수 명사 앞에만 붙일 수 있어요!

We buy a book for Mina. 우리는 미나에게 책을 사 준다.

부정관사 'a' 자음 소리로 시작되는 명사 앞

a cake 케이크

a hat 모자

부정관사 'an' 모음(a, e, i, o, u) 소리로 시작되는 명사 앞

an egg 계란

an hour 시간

hour, honest의 h는 소리 나지 않는 묵음이므로 an을 써요.

❖ POiNT 2 ❖

- **단, 명사 앞에 형용사가 오면 형용사의 첫 소리에 따라 a나 an을 써요!**

  a fresh egg 신선한 달걀 an easy book 쉬운 책 an honest boy 정직한 소년

- **다음 명사의 앞에는 부정관사를 쓰지 않아요.**

  a sugar (x) (셀 수 없는 명사) a Seoul (x) (고유명사)
  a dogs (x) (복수명사) an your pen (x) (소유격)

Check and Write

다음 [ ] 에 알맞은 부정관사를 넣어보세요. (부정관사를 쓸 수 없는 경우엔 ×표 하세요.)

1. 

[an] eraser

2. 

[ ] book

3. 

[ ] umbrella

4. 

[ ] elephant

5. 

[ ] cheetah

6. 

[ ] cat

7. 

[ ] water

8. 

[ ] orange

9. 

[ ] dogs

10. 

[ ] apple

11. 

[ ] ball

12. 

[ ] animals

정답과 해설 p.5

UNIT 02 정관사

The bike is old.

❖ POiNT 1 ❖

정관사 the의 '정'이라는 말은 '정해졌다'라는 뜻이에요.

특정한 사람 또는 사물을 가리키는 명사 앞에는 정관사 the를 써요.
어떤 대상에 대해 처음 말할 때는 부정관사 a/an을 쓰지만, 그 대상을 다시 말할 때는 정관사 the를 써요.

I have a bike. The bike is old. 나는 자전거가 (하나) 있어. 그 자전거는 낡았어.

❖ POiNT 2 ❖

정관사 the만 붙이는 명사

세상에 하나밖에 없는 명사

the sun 태양
the moon 달
the earth 지구
the sky 하늘

악기 명사

the piano 피아노 the violin 바이올린
※ 연주와 관련될 때 the를 써요.

위치나 방향

the right 오른쪽 the left 왼쪽
the east 동쪽 the west 서쪽

❖ POiNT 3 ❖

이럴 때는 정관사를 쓰지 않아요!

- 운동 이름 앞에 baseball 야구 basketball 농구 soccer 축구
  They play baseball together. 그들은 함께 야구를 한다.
- 과목 이름 앞에 math 수학 science 과학 history 역사
  Sihu studies history. 시후는 역사를 공부한다.
- 식사 이름 앞에 breakfast 아침 lunch 점심 dinner 저녁
  I have breakfast every day. 나는 매일 아침을 먹는다.
- 언어 이름 앞에 English 영어 Japanese 일본어 Chinese 중국어
  Many people learn Chinese. 많은 사람들이 중국어를 배운다.

정관사를 쓰지 않는 표현들

go home 집에 가다 go to school 학교에 가다 at home 집에서

Check and Write

각 문장의 [ ]에 알맞은 관사를 보기에서 골라 쓰세요. (관사를 쓸 수 없는 경우엔 ×표 하세요.)

보기 a an the

1. Today was [×] Mina's birthday.
오늘은 미나의 생일이었어.

2. [ ] sun was very shiny.
해가 아주 빛났어.

3. Mina's friends gave Mina [ ] cake.
미나의 친구들은 미나에게 케이크 하나를 주었어.

4. [ ] cake was delicious.
그 케이크는 맛있었어.

5. Mina played [ ] piano for her friends.
미나는 그녀의 친구들을 위해 피아노를 연주했어.

6. Then, they had [ ] dinner together.
그러고 나서 그들은 함께 저녁을 먹었어.

7. After dinner, her friends went [ ] home.
저녁식사 후에, 그녀의 친구들은 집에 갔어.

8. [ ] moon was very bright.
달이 참 밝았어.

정답과 해설 p.5

Practice 1 정관사와 부정관사의 알맞은 쓰임을 익혀 보아요.

다음 문장에 알맞은 명사를 보기에서 골라 어울리는 관사(a/an/the)와 함께 빈칸에 쓰세요. 관사가 필요 없을 경우 ×표 하세요. (단, 한 단어를 여러 번 쓸 수 있어요.)

A Nayeon is not happy.

보기 picture math English piano student

1. I saw ___a___ ___picture___. 나는 사진 한 장을 봤다.
2. ______ ______ was of me when I was young. I had no worries, then... (*worry: 걱정)
   그 사진은 어릴 때의 나였다. 저 때는 아무런 걱정이 없었는데…

3. Now, I am ______ ______. 이제, 난 학생이다.
   I have many duties. 내게는 많은 의무가 있다. (*duty: 의무)
4. I have to study ______ ______ and ______ ______.
   나는 수학과 영어를 공부해야 한다.
5. I just want to play ______ ______. 나는 그냥 피아노를 치고 싶다.

B I love my pet!

보기 dog family cat

1. I have ______ ______. 나는 개 한 마리를 가지고 있어.
2. ______ ______ is so cute. His name is Dubu.
   그 개는 정말 귀여워. 그의 이름은 두부야.
3. I have ______ ______. 나는 고양이 한 마리가 있어.

4. ______ ______ is shy. Her name is Mori.
   그 고양이는 수줍음이 많아. 그녀의 이름은 모리야.
5. They live with my ______ ______.
   그들은 내 가족과 함께 살아.

정답과 해설 p.5

C A birthday present

보기 doll cake hair clip necklace

1. Let's buy ______ ______ for Nayeon's birthday!
   나연이의 생일을 위해 케이크를 사자!

2. Sihu gives ______ ______ to Nayeon.
   시후가 나연이에게 인형을 준다.

3. ______ ______ is pretty. 그 인형은 예쁘다.

4. Mina wants ______ ______ for her birthday.
   미나는 생일 선물로 목걸이를 원한다.

5. Mina gets ______ ______ ______ for her birthday present. 미나는 생일 선물로 머리핀을 받는다.

D It's raining!

보기 coat umbrella muffler

1. It is raining. I need ______ ______.
   비가 와요. 나는 우산이 필요해요.

2. You have ______ ______. 너는 우산이 하나 있잖아.

3. I lost ______ ______ the other day.
   나는 그 우산을 전에 잃어버렸어요.

4. It will be cold tomorrow.
   I need ______ ______ and ______ ______.
   내일 추울 거예요. 나는 목도리와 코트가 필요해요.

5. I lost my ______ ______,too. 나는 내 목도리도 잃어버렸어요.

정답과 해설 p.5

Practice 2 명사에 알맞은 관사를 써서 문장을 완성해 보아요.

다음 우리말 뜻과 같도록 (   ) 안에 주어진 명사에 알맞은 관사를 붙여 문장을 완성하세요. (단, 관사가 필요 없을 경우 명사를 그대로 쓰세요.)

1. (moon) rises at night. 달은 밤에 뜬다.
   ➔ The moon rises at night.

2. Look at (sky). It is so beautiful! 하늘을 좀 봐. 정말 아름답다!
   ➔ Look at ______________. It is so beautiful!

3. Did you see (sun) and (moon) at the same time?
   너는 해와 달을 동시에 봤니?
   ➔ Did you see ______________ and ______________ at the same time?

4. I am at (home) on Sunday. 나는 일요일에 집에 있어.
   ➔ I am at ______________ on Sunday.

5. We fight over the bathroom before we go to (school). (*bathroom: 화장실)
   우리는 학교 가기 전에 화장실을 가지고 싸운다.
   ➔ We fight over the bathroom before we go to ______________.

6. You use the bathroom after you have (breakfast)!
   너는 아침 먹은 후에 화장실을 써!
   ➔ You use the bathroom after you have ______________!

7. If I don't wear my glasses, I'm as blind as (bat). (*blind: 눈이 먼)
   만약 내가 안경을 쓰지 않는다면, 나는 박쥐만큼 앞이 보이지 않아.
   ➔ If I don't wear my glasses, I'm as blind as ______________.

8. There is a cap on the suitcase. (hat) is white.
   여행가방 위에 모자 하나가 있다. 그 모자는 흰색이다.
   ➔ There is a cap on the suitcase. ______________ is white.

정답과 해설 p.5

9. I know (girl). (girl) is kind. 나는 한 여자 아이를 알아. 그 여자 아이는 친절해.

➜ I know ______________. ______________ is kind.

10. It's on (left). 그것은 왼쪽에 있어요.

➜ It's on ______________.

11. *A*: I want (chocolate)! 저 초콜릿을 원해요!

B: Ok. Here you are. 알겠어. 여기 있어.

➜ *A*: I want ______________!

B: Ok. Here you are.

12. I go to (Busan) every summer. 나는 매 여름마다 부산에 가.

➜ I go to ______________ every summer.

13. I have (apple). (apple) is in the basket.

나는 사과 한 개가 있어. 그 사과는 바구니 안에 있어.

➜ I have ______________. ______________ is in the basket.

14. 

(sky) is awake, so I'm awake, so we have to play! (*awake: 깨어 있는)

하늘이 깨어있어서 나도 깨어 있어, 그러니까 우린 놀아야 해!

➜ ______________ is awake, so I'm awake, so we have to play!

15. 

(pet) is an animal you don't eat.

애완동물은 네가 먹지 않는 동물이야.

➜ ______________ is an animal you don't eat.

정답과 해설 p.5

16. 

(hero) need not speak. When he is gone, (world) will speak for him.
영웅은 말할 필요가 없어. 그가 떠날 때, 세계가 그를 대신해 말할 거야.

➔ ______________ need not speak. When he is gone, ______________ will speak for him.

17. 

(dog) doesn't try to give advice or judge you. (*advice: 조언, judge: 판단하다)
개는 너에게 조언을 하거나 너를 판단하려고 하지 않아.

➔ ______________ doesn't try to give advice or judge you.

18. 

(dream) is (wish) your heart makes.
꿈은 당신의 마음이 만드는 소망이에요.

➔ ______________ is ______________ your heart makes.

19. 
[피카소]

Every child is (artist). 모든 아이들은 예술가다.
➔ Every child is ______________.

20. (good neighbor) is a priceless treasure. (*priceless: 값을 매길 수 없는)
좋은 이웃은 값을 매길 수 없는 보물이다.

➔ ________________________ is a priceless treasure.

정답과 해설 p.5

Practice 3 알맞은 관사와 명사를 써서 완전한 문장을 써 보아요.

우리말 뜻을 참고하여 빈칸에 알맞은 관사와 명사를 쓰고 완전한 영어문장을 써 보세요. (단, 관사가 필요 없을 경우 그대로 쓰세요.)

CH 02

1. I want ___a piano___. 난 피아노를 원해요.
   ➜ ___I want a piano___.

2. You cannot play ________. 너 피아노 칠 줄 모르잖아.
   ➜ ________________.

3. Look out ________. It is raining! 창문 밖을 봐. 비가 오고 있어!
   ➜ ________________. It is raining!

4. No way! I don't have ________! 말도 안 돼! 나 우산 없는데!
   ➜ No way! ________________!

5. Do you have ________? 너 우산 있니?
   ➜ ________________?

6. ________ does not shine. The ground is wet.
   해가 빛나지 않아. 땅이 축축해.
   ➜ ________________.
   The ground is wet.

7. When I get up late, I run to ________. 나는 늦게 일어나면, 학교에 뛰어간다.
   ➜ When I get up late, ________________.

8. There was ________ at the crosswalk.
   횡단보도에서 어떤 사고가 났다.
   ➜ ________________.

정답과 해설 p.5

9. Can you play ______________?

너 바이올린을 연주할 수 있니?

➜ ______________________

______________________?

10. I have ______________ with my computer. 내 컴퓨터에 어떤 문제가 있어.

➜ ______________________

______________________.

11. I heard ______________ today. 나 오늘 농담 하나를 들었어.

➜ ____.

12. ______________ was very funny. 그 농담은 매우 재미있었어.

➜ ____.

13. I had ______________ yesterday. 어제 나는 점심을 먹었다.

➜ ____.

14. He often plays ______________. 그는 종종 축구를 한다.

➜ ____.

15. Mina goes ______________ early because she has a cold.

미나는 감기에 걸렸기 때문에 일찍 집에 간다.

➜ ____.

정답과 해설 p.5

16. ______________ doesn't try to give advice or judge you.
개는 너에게 조언을 하거나 너를 판단하려고 하지 않아.

➔ ____.

17. ______________ is a good friend. 애완동물은 좋은 친구이다.

➔ ____.

18. Mom bought me a new bike. ______________ is really cool.
엄마가 나에게 새로운 자전거를 사주셨다. 그 자전거는 정말 멋지다.

➔ Mom bought me a new bike.

______________________________________.

19. I have ______________ for you. 나 너한테 줄 선물이 하나 있어.

➔ ____.

20. Dad bought me a pair of gloves. ______________ are very warm.
아빠가 나에게 장갑 한 켤레를 사주셨다. 그 장갑은 매우 따뜻하다.

➔ Dad bought me a pair of gloves.

______________________________________.

정답과 해설 p.5

Let's Practice More!

SET 01

학습목표 1 | a[an]의 알맞은 쓰임에 대해 알아보아요.　　공부한 날 :　　맞은 개수 :　　/12개

다음 문장의 빈칸에 a, an 중 알맞은 것을 쓰고, 필요 없는 곳에는 ×표 하세요.

01. It will be cold tomorrow. I need ___a___ muffler. 내일 추울 거야. 나는 머플러가 필요해.

02. It is raining. I need ________ umbrella.
비가 내리는 중이야. 나는 우산이 필요해.

03. I lost ________ books. 나는 책들을 잃어버렸어.

04. Mina gives ________ eraser to Minsu. 미나는 민수에게 지우개를 준다.

05. I know ________ honest boy. 나는 한 정직한 소년을 안다.

06. Mina got ________ hair clip for her birthday present. 미나는 생일 선물로 머리핀을 받았다.

07. I saw ________ picture of me. 나는 나의 사진 한 장을 봤다.

08. Now, I am ________ student. 이제, 나는 학생이다.

09. I have ________ duties. 나에게는 의무들이 있다.

10. ________ pet is a good friend.
애완동물은 좋은 친구이다.

11. They live with ________ my family. 그들은 내 가족과 함께 산다.

12. I have ________ present for you. 나 너한테 줄 선물이 하나 있어.

정답과 해설 p.5

Let's Practice More!

SET 02

학습목표 1 | a[an]의 알맞은 쓰임에 대해 알아보아요. 공부한 날 : 맞은 개수 : /14개

CH 02

다음 문장의 빈칸에 a, an 중 알맞은 것을 쓰고, 필요 없는 곳에는 ×표 하세요.

01. She is ___an___ English teacher. 그녀는 영어 선생님이다.

02. ________ dream is a wish your heart makes. 꿈은 당신의 마음이 만드는 소망이에요.

03. Every child is ________ artist. 모든 아이들은 예술가이다.

04. I lost ________ umbrella the other day. 나는 우산 하나를 전에 잃어버렸다.

05. I argued with my sister for ________ hour.
나는 내 동생과 한 시간 동안 다퉜다.

06. ________ apple is in the basket. 사과 한 개가 바구니 안에 있어.

07. Sihu gives ________ doll to Nayeon. 시후가 나연이에게 인형을 준다.

08. A pet is ________ animal you don't eat. 애완동물은 네가 먹지 않는 동물이야.

09. Now, I'm ________ your guest. 지금, 나는 너의 손님이야.

10. I have ________ message for you.
나는 너를 위한 메시지가 하나 있어.(나는 너에게 전할 메시지가 하나 있어.)

11. No way! I don't have ________ umbrella! 말도 안 돼! 나는 우산이 없어!

12. I have ________ problem with my computer. 내 컴퓨터에 어떤 문제가 있어.

13. My cousin is ________ honest boy. 내 사촌은 정직한 소년이다.

14. I saw ________ picture of ________ handsome man.
나는 한 잘생긴 남자의 사진을 봤다.

정답과 해설 p.5

Let's Practice More!

SET 03

학습목표 1 | a[an]의 알맞은 쓰임에 대해 알아보아요. 공부한 날 : 맞은 개수 : /14개

다음 문장의 빈칸에 a, an 중 알맞은 것을 쓰고, 필요 없는 곳에는 ×표 하세요.

01. I'm as fast as ___a___ cheetah. 나는 치타만큼 빠르다.

02. ________ good neighbor is a priceless treasure. 좋은 이웃은 값을 매길 수 없는 보물이다.

03. I saw ________ picture on the wall. 나는 벽에 있는 사진 한 장을 봤다.

04. There was ________ accident at the crosswalk. 횡단보도에서 어떤 사고가 났다.

05. Mom took me to ________ doctor. 엄마는 나를 한 의사에게 데리고 갔다.

06. I have ________ cats. 나는 고양이들이 있다.

07. I heard ________ joke today. 나 오늘 농담 하나를 들었어.

08. There is ________ police officer on the crosswalk.
횡단보도에 경찰관 한 명이 있다.

09. ________ dog doesn't try to give advice. 개는 너에게 조언을 하려고 하지 않는다.

10. No way! I don't have any ________ money. 말도 안 돼! 나는 돈이 하나도 없어.

11. Do you have ________ umbrella? 너는 우산을 가지고 있니?

12. I argue with ________ my mother over little things. 나는 나의 엄마와 작은 일로 다툰다.

13. I read ________ easy book. 나는 쉬운 책을 읽었다.

14. Let's buy ________ cake for Mina's birthday.
미나의 생일을 위해 케이크를 하나 사자.

정답과 해설 p.5

Let's Practice More!

SET 04

학습목표 2 | the의 알맞은 쓰임에 대해 알아보아요. 공부한 날 : 맞은 개수 : /12개

다음 문장의 빈칸에 the가 필요한 곳에는 the를 쓰고, 필요 없는 곳에는 ×표 하세요.

01. ___The___ moon rises at night. 달은 밤에 뜬다.

02. There is a cap on the suitcase. ________ cap is white.
여행 가방 위에 모자가 하나 있다. 그 모자는 하얀색이다.

03. We fight in the classroom before we go ________ home.
우리는 집에 가기 전에 교실에서 싸운다.

04. I can speak ________ English. 나는 영어를 할 수 있다.

05. ________ sky is awake. 하늘이 깨어있어.

06. I played ________ piano last night. 나는 지난밤에 피아노를 쳤어.

07. I have a cat. ________ cat is cute.
나는 고양이 한 마리가 있어. 그 고양이는 귀여워.

08. I have ________ breakfast. 나는 아침을 먹어.

09. Mom bought me a new computer. ________ computer is really cool.
엄마는 나에게 새로운 컴퓨터를 하나 사주셨어. 그 컴퓨터는 진짜 멋져.

10. I have to study ________ math. 나는 수학을 공부해야 해.

11. You cannot play ________ violin. 너는 바이올린을 켤 수 없어.

12. When I get up late, I run to ________ school. 내가 늦게 일어날 때, 나는 학교로 달려간다.

정답과 해설 p.6

Let's Practice More!

SET 05

학습목표 2 | the의 알맞은 쓰임에 대해 알아보아요. 공부한 날 : 맞은 개수 : /14개

다음 문장의 빈칸에 the가 필요한 곳에는 the를 쓰고, 필요 없는 곳에는 ×표 하세요.

01. She studies ____×____ history. 그녀는 역사를 공부한다.

02. Do you see __________ snowman? 너는 그 눈사람을 보니?

03. __________ sun does not shine. 해가 빛나지 않아.

04. We go to __________ school. 우리는 학교에 간다.

05. Dad bought me a pair of gloves.
__________ gloves are very warm.
아빠가 나에게 장갑 한 켤레를 사주셨어. 그 장갑은 매우 따뜻해.

06. The sun rises in __________ east. 해는 동쪽에서 뜬다.

07. __________ joke was very funny. 그 농담은 매우 재미있었어.

08. Look at __________ moon. It is so beautiful! 달을 좀 봐. 매우 아름다워!

09. I want to play __________ piano. 나는 피아노를 치고 싶어.

10. We are playing __________ baseball. 우리는 야구를 하는 중이야.

11. Look out __________ window. It is raining! 창문 밖을 좀 봐. 비가 내리고 있어!

12. It's on __________ left. 그것은 왼쪽에 있어.

13. I have a bike. __________ bike is old.
나는 자전거가 하나 있어. 그 자전거는 오래됐어.

14. I have a doll. __________ doll is very cute.
나는 인형 하나가 있어. 그 인형은 매우 귀여워.

정답과 해설 p.6

Let's Practice More!

SET 06

학습목표 2 | the의 알맞은 쓰임에 대해 알아보아요. 공부한 날 : 맞은 개수 : /14개

다음 문장의 빈칸에 the가 필요한 곳에는 the를 쓰고, 필요 없는 곳에는 ×표 하세요.

01. I have to learn ____×____ English. 나는 영어를 배워야 한다.

02. Do you see ________ sun and ________ moon at the same time?
너는 태양과 달을 동시에 보니?

03. Mina goes ________ home early because she has a cold.
미나는 감기에 걸렸기 때문에 일찍 집에 간다.

04. We took a trip. ________ trip was great.
우리는 여행을 갔어. 그 여행은 멋졌어.

05. Jisu and Sihu study ________ math together. 지수와 시후는 같이 수학을 공부한다.

06. ________ sun sets in the west. 해는 서쪽으로 진다.

07. Will you play ________ soccer this afternoon?
오늘 오후에 축구할래?

08. My friend plays ________ piano very well. 내 친구는 피아노를 매우 잘 친다.

09. Many people learn ________ Chinese. 많은 사람들은 중국어를 배운다.

10. Dad bought me a new computer. ________ computer is really good.
아빠는 나에게 새로운 컴퓨터를 하나 사주셨어. 그 컴퓨터는 진짜 좋아.

11. My family has ________ dinner every night. 나의 가족은 매일 밤 저녁을 먹는다.

12. Do you see ________ picture? 너는 그 사진을 보니?

13. She is reading a book. ________ book is interesting.
그녀는 책을 읽는 중이야. 그 책은 흥미로워.

14. I play ________ piano every day. 나는 매일 피아노를 친다.

정답과 해설 p.6

Let's Practice More!

SET 07

학습목표 3 | a[an]와 the의 쓰임을 구별해 보아요.　　공부한 날 :　　맞은 개수 :　　/20개

우리말 뜻에 유의하여 빈칸에 적절한 표현을 넣어 영어문장을 완성해 보세요.

01. I must study ___science___.
나는 과학을 공부해야 한다.

02. ________ ________ ________ is a priceless treasure.
좋은 친구는 값을 매길 수 없는 보물이다.

03. My family has ________ together every day.
나의 가족은 매일 점심을 같이 먹는다.

04. Nayeon plays ________ ________ very well.
나연이는 피아노를 아주 잘 친다.

05. He is ________ ________ ________.
그는 정직한 소년이다.

06. She is reading a book. ________ ________ is interesting.
그녀는 책을 읽고 있다. 그 책은 흥미롭다.

07. ________ ________ doesn't try to judge you.
개는 너를 판단하려고 하지 않아.

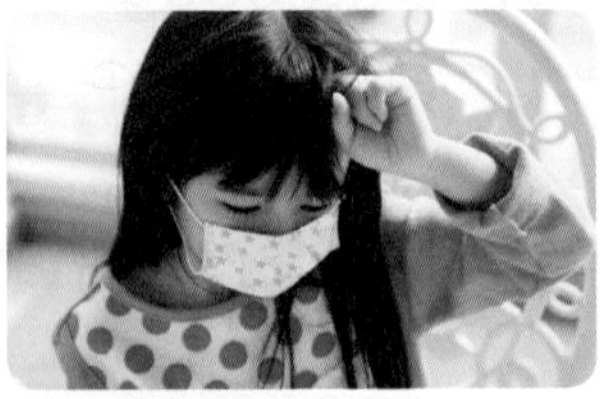

08. Mina goes ________ early because she has a cold.
미나는 감기에 걸렸기 때문에 일찍 집에 간다.

09. They took a trip. ________ ________ was great. (*trip: 여행)
그들은 여행을 떠났다. 그 여행은 매우 훌륭했다.

10. ________ ________ is really good.
그 컴퓨터는 정말로 좋다.

정답과 해설 p.6

11. The post office is on ______________ right.
그 우체국은 오른쪽에 있어.

12. There was ______________ ______________ at the crosswalk.
횡단보도에서 어떤 사고가 났다.

13. Did you see ______________ ______________ and ______________ ______________ at the same time?
너는 해와 달을 동시에 보았니?

14. I heard ______________ ______________ last night.
나 어젯밤에 농담 하나를 들었어.

15. No way! I don't have any ______________.
말도 안 돼! 나는 돈이 하나도 없어.

16. I argue with my ______________ over nothing.
나는 내 친구와 아무 것도 아닌 일로 다툰다.

17. Do you have ______________ ______________?
너 우산 하나 있니?

18. Mom took me to ______________ ______________.
엄마는 나를 한 의사에게 데리고 갔다.

19. The sun sets in ______________ ______________.
태양은 서쪽으로 진다.

20. We go to ______________ at 8 a.m.
우리는 아침 8시에 학교에 가.

정답과 해설 p.6

Let's Practice More!

SET 08

학습목표 3 | a[an]와 the의 쓰임을 구별해 보아요. 공부한 날 : 맞은 개수 : /20개

우리말 뜻에 유의하여 빈칸에 적절한 단어를 넣어 영어문장을 완성해 보세요.

01. I know ___an___ ___honest___ ___boy___.
나는 한 정직한 소년을 알아.

02. ________ ________ goes to school.
그 소년은 학교에 간다.

03. I lost my ________.
나는 내 책들을 잃어 버렸어.

04. I saw ________ ________.
나는 사진 한 장을 봤어.

05. A cheetah was in ________ ________.
그 사진에는 치타가 있었어.

06. Dad has ________ ________.
아빠는 목도리를 한 개 가지고 계셔.

07. Mina gives ________ ________ to Minsu.
미나가 지우개 하나를 민수에게 준다.

08. I need ________ ________ tomorrow.
나는 내일 그 우산이 필요해.

09. I have ________ ________ for you.
난 네게 줄 선물이 하나 있어.

10. ________ ________ is a cute hair clip.
그 선물은 귀여운 머리핀이야.

11. ________ ________ is a wish.
꿈은 소원이야.

정답과 해설 p.6

CH
02

12. Your heart makes ______________ ______________.
네 마음이 그 꿈을 만들지.

13. It is raining. I need ______________ ______________.
비가 내리는 중이야. 나는 우산이 한 개 필요해.

14. ______________ ______________ is in the basket.
사과 한 개가 바구니 안에 있어.

15. ______________ ______________ is so sweet.
그 사과는 정말 달콤해.

16. Every child is ______________ ______________.
모든 아이들은 예술가야.

17. ______________ ______________ paints pictures.
그 예술가는 그림을 그려.

18. Now, I am ______________ ______________.
이제 나는 학생이야.

19. I have ______________ ______________.
나는 개 한 마리를 가지고 있어.

20. ______________ ______________ is so cute. His name is Dubu.
그 개는 정말 귀여워. 그의 이름은 두부야.

정답과 해설 p.6

CHAPTER 01~02

실전테스트

공부한 날 :

복습한 날 :

부모님 확인 :

CHAPTER 01 명사 CHAPTER 02 관사

●정답과 해설은 별책 6쪽에서 확인하세요!!

01

다음 단어들 중 셀 수 있는 명사 두 개를 골라 ○표 하세요.

water, pen, bread, tree, juice

[02~04] 다음 그림을 보고, 빈칸에 들어갈 알맞은 알파벳을 쓰세요.

02

f i ☐ ☐

03

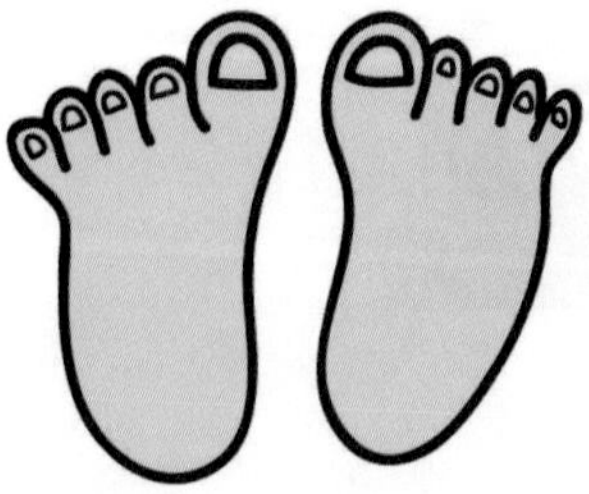

f ☐ ☐ t

04

l e a ☐ ☐ ☐

[05~09] 우리말 해석과 같도록 [보기]에서 알맞은 단어를 골라 빈칸에 쓰세요.

[보기] sheets loaf bar cup piece

05

He ate a __________ of chocolate.

(그는 초콜릿 바 하나를 먹었다.)

06

He bought a __________ of bread today.

(그는 오늘 빵 한 덩어리를 샀다.)

07

They ate a __________ of cake after dinner.

(그들은 저녁 식사 후에 케이크 한 조각을 먹었다.)

08

I drink a __________ of milk every morning.
(나는 매일 아침 우유 한 컵을 마신다.)

09

I have two __________ of paper.
(나는 종이 두 장을 가지고 있다.)

[10~11] 다음 단어 중 나머지 넷과 그 성격이 다른 명사에 ○표 하세요.

10

school, bank, museum, love, restaurant

11

apple, milk, water, money, cheese

[12~13] 다음 표의 빈칸에 [보기]의 단어를 분류해서 쓰세요.

12

[보기] milk, love, USA, family, bread, team, tree

셀 수 있는 명사	셀 수 없는 명사

13

[보기] water, hope, flower, egg, juice

셀 수 있는 명사	셀 수 없는 명사

[14~16] 다음 그림에 맞게 문장을 바르게 고치세요.

14

He has five dish.

→ ____________________

15

I want three box.

→ ____________________

16

Child hold their hands.

→ ______________________________

[17~19] 다음 주어진 그림과 단어를 보고, 알맞은 관사에 ○표 하세요.

17

(a, an) ant

18

(an, the) earth

19

(a, an) car

[20~23] 우리말 해석과 같도록 [보기]에서 알맞은 관사를 골라 빈칸에 쓰세요.

[보기] a, an, the

20

This is __________ notebook.

(이것은 공책이다.)

21

Look at __________ lion.

(그 사자를 봐라.)

22

__________ man is my uncle.

(그 남자가 나의 삼촌이다.)

23

I need __________ eraser.

(나는 지우개 한 개가 필요하다.)

[24~28] 다음 밑줄 친 부분을 바르게 고치고, 전체 문장을 쓰세요.

24

James reads <u>an</u> book.

⇨ ______________________________

25

She has two <u>childs</u>.

⇨ ______________________________

26

I play <u>a</u> piano on Monday.

⇨ ______________________________

27

My father eats three <u>tomatos</u>.

⇨ ______________________________

28

Do you like <u>fishes</u>?

⇨ ______________________________

[29~30] 다음 문장에서 잘못 쓴 부분을 찾아 바르게 고치세요.

29

<u>He</u>① <u>plays</u>② <u>a</u>③ <u>violin</u>④.

잘못 쓴 부분 : ____________________

고쳐 쓰기 : ____________________

30

<u>A</u>① <u>sun</u>② <u>sets</u>③ <u>in</u>④ <u>the</u>⑤ <u>west</u>⑥.

잘못 쓴 부분 : ____________________

고쳐 쓰기 : ____________________

Chapter 03 인칭대명사

이 챕터에서는 사람, 사물의 이름을 대신하여 쓰는 '인칭대명사'에 대해 익히고,
인칭대명사의 종류와 차이점에 대해 배워 봐요.

☆ 학습 방향 및 배울 내용 미리보기 ☆

☐ **Unit 01 : I** like Mina. **She** is kind.
주격 인칭대명사
주격 인칭대명사는 어느 때 쓰고, 어떤 형태인지 배워 봐요.

▼

☐ **Unit 02 :** I like Sihu. Many girls like **him**.
목적격 인칭대명사
목적격 인칭대명사는 어느 때 쓰고, 어떤 형태인지 배워 봐요.

▼

☐ **Unit 03 :** Hayul is **my** little brother.
소유격 인칭대명사
소유격 인칭대명사는 어느 때 쓰고, 어떤 형태인지 배워 봐요.

▼

☐ **Unit 04 :** It is now **yours**.
소유대명사
소유대명사는 어느 때 쓰고, 어떤 형태인지 배워 봐요.

단어 미리보기

이 챕터에 나올 단어들 중 이미 알고 있는 단어가 있나요?
맞는 뜻을 골라 체크해 봐요.

날짜 : 이름 : 알고 있는 단어의 수 : /24개

No.	아는 단어	단어	품사	알맞은 뜻에 체크 표시해 봐요.			
1	☑	cook	동사	요리하다	☑	찌르다	☐
2	☐	lovely	형용사	아름다운	☐	사랑스러운	☐
3	☐	son	명사	아들	☐	해	☐
4	☐	pencil	명사	연필	☐	볼펜	☐
5	☐	sing	동사	바람이 불다	☐	노래하다	☐
6	☐	tomorrow	명사	오늘	☐	내일	☐
7	☐	think	동사	알다	☐	생각하다	☐
8	☐	hero	명사	영웅	☐	왕	☐
9	☐	ring	명사	목걸이	☐	반지	☐
10	☐	voice	명사	남자아이	☐	목소리	☐
11	☐	first	형용사	둘째의	☐	첫째의	☐
12	☐	full	형용사	가득한	☐	빈	☐
13	☐	talk	동사	부수다	☐	말하다	☐
14	☐	put	동사	웃다	☐	놓다	☐
15	☐	number	명사	번호	☐	바지	☐
16	☐	pleasure	명사	기쁨	☐	슬픔	☐
17	☐	cut	동사	찍다	☐	자르다	☐
18	☐	notebook	명사	공책	☐	책상	☐
19	☐	secret	명사	경비	☐	비밀	☐
20	☐	smell	명사	방귀	☐	냄새	☐
21	☐	remember	동사	잊다	☐	기억하다	☐
22	☐	map	명사	지도	☐	길	☐
23	☐	bake	동사	굽다	☐	찌다	☐
24	☐	differently	부사	같게	☐	다르게	☐

주격 인칭대명사

UNIT 01 I like Mina. She is kind.

❖ POiNT 1 ❖

인칭대명사는 사람, 사물의 이름을 대신하여 쓰는 명사예요.

I like Mina. 나는 미나를 좋아해.

She is kind. 그녀는 상냥해.

❖ POiNT 2 ❖

주격 인칭대명사는 인칭대명사 중 주어를 대신해서 쓰는 것을 말해요.

주어가 말하는 사람일 때는 1인칭, 듣는 사람일 때는 2인칭, 다른 사람일 때는 3인칭이라고 해요!

한 명 / 한 개 (단수)	1인칭	**I** 나는	**I** walk my dog every day. 나는 내 개를 매일 산책시켜.
	2인칭	**You** 너는	**You** are a mess. 너는 꼴이 엉망이구나.
	3인칭	**He** 그는	**He** plays Minecraft. 그는 마인크래프트 게임을 해.
		She 그녀는	**She** has a fever. 그녀는 열이 나.
		It 그것은	**It** is awesome. 그것은 아주 멋져.
여러 명 / 여러 개 (복수)	1인칭	**We** 우리는	**We** ride our bikes after school. 우리는 방과 후에 자전거를 타.
	2인칭	**You** 너희들은	**You** are very cute. 너희들은 정말 귀여워.
	3인칭	**They** 그들은 그것들은	**They** are late for school. 그들은 학교에 늦었어.

Check and Write

다음 문장을 보고 [ ]에 알맞은 인칭대명사를 쓰세요.

1. Dad bought me a dog.
아빠는 나에게 개 한 마리를 사 주셨어.
[It] is so cute.
그것은 정말 귀여워.

2. My mom made me a cake.
엄마는 나에게 케이크를 만들어 주셨어.
[   ] cooks very well.
그녀는 요리를 매우 잘하셔.

3. I love my friends.
나는 내 친구들을 무척 좋아해.
[   ] are funny.
그들은 재미있어.

4. [   ] want to have a cat.
나는 고양이 한 마리를 가지고 싶어요.

5. [   ] have a dog.
너는 개 한 마리가 있잖아.

6. Mina is my classmate.
미나는 나의 학급친구야.
[   ] are best friends.
우리는 가장 친한 친구야.

7. [   ] are my lovely sons.
너희들은 나의 사랑스러운 아들들이다.

정답과 해설 p.6

UNIT 02 I like Sihu. Many girls like him.

❖ POiNT 1 ❖

I like Sihu. 나는 시후를 좋아해.

He is funny. 그는 재미있어.
(He: 주격 인칭대명사)

Many girls like him. 많은 소녀들이 그를 좋아해.
(him: 목적격 인칭대명사)

❖ POiNT 2 ❖

목적격 인칭대명사는 목적어를 대신해서 써요.

한 명 / 한 개 (단수)	1인칭	**me** 나를	He knows **me**! 그가 나를 알아!
	2인칭	**you** 너를	I remember **you**. 난 너를 기억해.
	3인칭	**him** 그를	Sandra likes **him** very much. Sandra는 그를 매우 좋아해.
		her 그녀를	Nick always teases **her**. Nick은 항상 그녀를 놀려. (*tease: 놀리다)
		it 그것을	I don't forget **it**. 나는 그것을 잊지 않아.
여러 명 / 여러 개 (복수)	1인칭	**us** 우리를	Mr. Kim teaches **us**. 김 선생님은 우리를 가르치셔.
	2인칭	**you** 너희들을	I need **you**. 난 너희들을 필요로 해.
	3인칭	**them** 그들을 그것들을	She hates **them**. 그녀는 그것들을 싫어해.

Check and Write

다음 문장을 보고 ______에 들어갈 알맞은 인칭대명사를 쓰세요.

1. Dad bought me a dog.
   아빠는 나에게 개 한 마리를 사주셨어.

   I love it. 나는 그것을 아주 좋아해.

2. Mina lends me a book.
   미나는 나에게 책 한 권을 빌려준다.

   I will give it back to ______.
   나는 그것을 그녀에게 돌려줄거야.

3. Mom likes vegetables very much.
   엄마는 채소를 매우 좋아하셔.

   But I hate ______.
   하지만 나는 그것들을 싫어해.

4. Exercise is good for ______.
   운동은 우리에게 좋아.

5. I have a present for ______.
   나는 널 위한 선물이 있어.

6. Mina gave ______ a gift.
   미나는 나에게 선물을 줬어.

정답과 해설 p.6

Practice 1 상황에 맞는 적절한 인칭대명사를 익혀 보아요.

다음 문장에 알맞은 인칭대명사를 보기 에서 골라 빈칸 안에 쓰세요. (단, 한 단어는 여러 번 쓸 수 있어요.)

A My birthday party

보기 I me We it They

1. On my birthday, _____I_____ will have a pajama party.
내 생일에 나는 파자마 파티를 할 것이다.

2. __________ invited three friends, Mina, Jihyo and Yuri.
나는 친구 세 명을 초대했는데, 미나, 지효와 유리이다.

3. __________ are my best friends.
그들은 나의 가장 친한 친구들이다.

4. __________ are going to watch a movie at night. 우리는 밤에 영화를 볼 것이다.

5. My mom bought an ice cream cake for __________.
나의 엄마는 날 위해 아이스크림 케이크를 하나 사셨다.

6. I really want to taste __________. I can't wait!
나는 정말 그걸 맛보고 싶다. 정말 기대된다!

B My brother is selfish!

보기 He[he] him me it them

1. My mom bought __________ some colored pencils. 나의 엄마가 나에게 색연필 몇 자루를 사 주셨다.

2. My brother said __________ needed __________, too.
내 남동생은 그도 그것들이 필요하다고 말했다.

정답과 해설 p.6

3. Now, I have to share __________ with __________.
이제 나는 그것들을 그와 같이 써야 한다.

4. I asked __________, "Can I borrow your pencil sharpener?"
나는 그에게 "내가 너의 연필깎이를 빌릴 수 있을까?"라고 물었다.

5. But he does not lend __________ to me.
그런데 그는 나에게 그것을 빌려주지 않는다.

6. __________ is so selfish! 그는 너무 이기적이다!

C My little sister's birthday is in a few days.

보기 she[She] her it them

1. My little sister's birthday is this Saturday, and __________ really likes "My Little Pony."
내 여동생의 생일이 이번 토요일인데 그녀는 '마이 리틀 포니'를 정말 좋아한다.

2. __________ is a big fan of __________ . 그녀는 그것의 열렬한 팬이다.

3. __________ watches __________ all the time. 그녀는 항상 그것을 본다.

4. So, I will give __________ a "My Little Pony" coloring book and crayons. 그래서 나는 그녀에게 '마이 리틀 포니' 색칠공부 책과 크레용을 줄 것이다.

5. I hope __________ likes __________. 나는 그녀가 그것들을 좋아하길 바란다.

D Tone-deaf (*tone-deaf: 음치의)

보기 I Me you

1. *Sihu* : Do __________ like singing? 너 노래하는 것 좋아해?

2. *Junwoo* : No. __________ am tone-deaf.
아니. 난 음치야.

3. *Sihu* : __________ too. 나도 그래.

정답과 해설 p.6

Practice 2 인칭대명사를 써서 문장을 완성해 보아요.

다음 우리말 뜻과 같도록 주어진 표현을 순서에 맞게 배열하여 문장을 완성하세요.

1. Jinho is tone-deaf. (cannot, He, carry a tune).
   진호는 음치야. 그는 음정을 맞추질 못해.
   ➔ Jinho is tone-deaf. He cannot carry a tune.

2. Yuri is a great singer. (envy, her, I). 유리는 훌륭한 가수야. 난 그녀가 부러워.
   ➔ Yuri is a great singer. ______________.

3. It is my birthday today. (I, thirteen, am turning)!
   오늘은 내 생일이다. 나는 13살이 된다!
   ➔ It is my birthday today.
   ______________!

4. I had Jinho and Sihu over. (my, They, best friends, are).
   나는 진호와 시후에게 놀러오라고 했다. 그들은 나의 가장 친한 친구들이다.
   ➔ I had Jinho and Sihu over. ______________.

5. (a stuffed cat, gives, Jinho, me). (*stuffed cat: 고양이 인형)
   진호는 나에게 고양이 인형을 준다.
   ➔ ______________.

6. (fluffy, was, so, It). (*fluffy: 보송보송한)
   그것은 매우 보송보송했다.
   ➔ ______________.

7. (I, "Meow," it, named). 나는 그것에게 '야옹이'라고 이름을 지어주었다.
   ➔ ______________.

정답과 해설 p.6

8. (colored pencils, Sihu, me, gives). 시후는 나에게 색연필들을 준다.

➔ ______________________________.

9. (I, "Meow," with, will draw, them). 나는 그것들로 '야옹이'를 그릴 것이다.

➔ ______________________________.

10. After dinner, (had, a chocolate cake, we).
저녁식사 후에, 우리는 초콜릿 케이크를 먹었다.

➔ After dinner, ______________________________.

11. (was, really delicious, It). 그것은 정말 맛있었다.

➔ ______________________________.

12. I want to (tomorrow, again, eat it). 나는 내일 그걸 또 먹고 싶다.

➔ I want to ______________________________.

13. (your friends, not really, are, They).
그들은 진짜 너의 친구들이 아니야.

➔ ______________________________

______________________________.

14. The world is not in your books or maps. (out there, is, It). 세상은 너의 책이나 지도 안에 있는 게 아냐. 그건 저 밖에 있어.

➔ The world is not in your books or maps.

____

______________________________.

정답과 해설 p.7

15. If you want something done, (must do, it, yourself, you).
네가 무언가가 이루어지길 바란다면, 너는 그것을 직접 해야 한다.

➔ If you want something done,
____.

16. Teenagers... They think (everything, know, they)
10대들이란... 그들은 자기들이 모든 걸 다 안다고 생각한다니까.

➔ Teenagers... They think
____
________________________.

17. When he is gone, (will speak for, the world, him).
그가 사라지면, 세상이 그를 대변할 것이다.

➔ When he is gone,
____
________________________.

18. Once we accept our limits, (go, beyond, we, them). (*beyond: (능력 · 한계 등을) 넘어서는)
우리가 우리의 한계를 인정하고 나면, 우리는 그것들을 넘어선다. [알버트 아인슈타인]

➔ Once we accept our limits, ____.

19. Life is not fair. (to, Get, it, used). 인생은 공평하지 않다. 그것에 익숙해져라. [빌 게이츠]

➔ Life is not fair. ____.

20. (the courage to pursue it, We, have). 우리는 그것을 좇으려는 용기가 있다. [월트 디즈니]

➔ ____.

정답과 해설 p.7

Practice 3 인칭대명사가 쓰인 문장을 완성해 보아요.

우리말 뜻을 참고하여 다음 주어진 표현을 사용해 문장을 완성해 보세요.

1. (watched, "Superstar K", last night) 나는 어젯밤에 '슈퍼스타K'를 봤어.

→ I watched "Superstar K" last night.

2. (want to be, like) 천단비가 멋졌어. 나는 그녀처럼 되고 싶어. (*like: ~처럼)

→ Danbi Cheon was wonderful. ______________________.

3. (want to get, something special, for) (*for: ~를 위해)

오늘은 내 남동생의 생일이다. 나는 그를 위해 특별한 무언가를 주고 싶다.

→ Today is my brother's birthday.

______________________.

4. (loves, "Kung Fu Panda") 그는 '쿵푸팬더'를 정말 좋아한다.

→ ______________________.

5. (will give, a stuffed panda) (*stuffed panda: 판다 인형)

나는 그에게 판다 인형을 줄 것이다.

→ ______________________

______________________.

6. (likes) 나는 그가 그것을 좋아하길 바란다. (*hope: 바라다)

→ I hope (that) ______________________.

7. (My mom, bakes, cookies, for) 나의 엄마는 나를 위해 쿠키를 구우신다.

→ ______________________.

정답과 해설 p.7

8. (called, best friend, Mina) 나는 나의 가장 친한 친구인 미나에게 전화했다.

➜ ____.

9. (smell delicious)

그것들은 맛있는 냄새가 난다.

➜ ______________________

______________________.

10. (Share, with me)

나랑 그것들을 나눠먹자.

➜ ______________________

______________________.

11. (have, together) 우리는 함께 그것들을 먹는다.

➜ ____.

12. (packed, for her brother) 나는 그녀의 남동생을 위해 그것들을 싸 주었다.

➜ ____.

13. (does not allow, to play mobile games) (*allow A to V: A가 ~하도록 허락하다)

그녀는 내가 모바일 게임을 하지 못하게 한다.

➜ ____.

14. (is, fair) 나는 그것이 공평하다고 생각하지 않는다.

➜ I don't think ______________________________.

정답과 해설 p.7

15. (will play, with my smartphone) 당신이 TV를 볼 때 나는 내 스마트폰을 갖고 놀게요.

➔ ______________________________ when you watch TV.

16. (Suho, treats, differently) 수호는 나를 다르게 대한다.

➔ ____.

17. (watches, a TV series, every night)
그녀는 매일 밤 텔레비전 연속물을 본다.

➔ ____________________
____________________.

18. (loves)
내 생각에 그는 나를 사랑하는 것 같다.

➔ I think that __________
____________________.

19. (the world, will, speak for) (*speak for: ~를 대변하다)
그가 사라지면, 세상이 그를 대변할 것이다.

➔ When he is gone, ______________________________.

20. (have the courage to pursue) (*pursue: ~을 추구하다)
우리가 그것들을 추구할 용기를 가진다면 우리의 모든 꿈은 이루어질 수 있다.

➔ All our dreams can come true if ______________________________.

정답과 해설 p.7

Let's Practice More!

SET 01

학습목표 1 | 주격 인칭대명사(I, You, He, She, It, We, They)를 익혀 보아요.　　공부한 날 :　　맞은 개수 :　　/12개

다음 우리말 뜻에 맞는 1인칭 주격 인칭대명사(I, We)를 빈칸에 넣어 보세요.

01. ___I___ have a pajama party today. 난 오늘 파자마 파티가 있다.

02. ________ am tone-deaf. 난 음치야.

03. ________ invite many friends. 우리는 많은 친구들을 초대한다.

04. ________ have the courage. 우리에겐 용기가 있다.

05. ________ want to go home. 난 집에 가고 싶다.

06. ________ will watch a movie. 우리는 영화를 볼 것이다.

07. ________ named it "Meow." 난 그것을 '야옹이'라 이름 붙였다.

08. ________ really want to taste it. 난 정말 그것을 맛보고 싶다.

09. ________ eat cookies together. 우리는 함께 쿠키를 먹는다.

10. ________ ride our bikes after school.
우리는 방과 후에 자전거를 탄다.

11. ________ can't live without him. 나는 그 없이는 살 수 없다.

12. ________ am turning thirteen. 나는 열세 살이 된다.

정답과 해설 p.7

Let's Practice More!

SET 02

학습목표 1 | 주격 인칭대명사(I, You, He, She, It, We, They)를 익혀 보아요.　공부한 날 :　맞은 개수 : /14개

다음 문장의 2인칭 주격 인칭대명사 You[you]가 단수인지 복수인지 쓰세요.

01. You must do it yourself. → 단수

02. You don't need to speak, Sihu. → ________

03. You are my lovely sons. → ________

04. You are very kind, Mina. → ________

05. You are good students. → ________

06. You are my best friends. → ________

07. You sing very well, Mina. → ________

08. You are bad boys. → ________

09. Sihu, you must share it with your sister. → ________

10. You are a big fan of "Kung Fu Panda." → ________

11. You play soccer together after school. → ________

12. Sihu, I think you like Mina. → ________

13. You always eat lunch together. → ________

14. You are a bad singer. → ________

정답과 해설 p.7

Let's Practice More!

SET 03

학습목표 1 | 주격 인칭대명사(I, You, He, She, It, We, They)를 익혀 보아요. 공부한 날 : 맞은 개수 : /14개

다음 우리말 뜻에 맞는 3인칭 주격 인칭대명사(He, She, It, They)를 빈칸에 쓰세요.

01. He is so selfish. 그는 너무 이기적이다.

02. ________ likes "My Little Pony."
그녀는 '마이 리틀 포니'를 좋아한다.

03. ________ is so fluffy. 그것은 (털이) 매우 보송보송하다.

04. ________ cannot carry a tune. 그는 음정을 맞추지 못한다.

05. ________ smell delicious. 그것들은 맛있는 냄새가 난다.

06. ________ watches TV every night. 그녀는 매일 밤 TV를 본다.

07. ________ was really delicious. 그것은 정말 맛있었다.

08. ________ has a fever. 그는 열이 있다.

09. ________ is a big fan of it. 그녀는 그것의 열성적인 팬이다.

10. ________ know everything. 그들은 모든 것을 알고 있다.

11. ________ loves "Kung Fu Panda." 그는 '쿵푸팬더'를 아주 좋아한다.

12. ________ is not fair. 그건 공평하지 않다.

13. ________ bakes cookies. 그녀는 쿠키를 굽는다.

14. ________ are my best friends.
그들은 나의 가장 친한 친구들이다.

정답과 해설 p.7

Let's Practice More!

SET 04

학습목표 2 | 목적격 인칭대명사(me, you, him, her, it, us, them)를 익혀 보아요.

공부한 날 : 맞은 개수 : /12개

다음 우리말 뜻에 맞는 1인칭 목적격 인칭대명사(me, us)를 빈칸에 쓰세요.

01. Mom bakes cookies for ___us___. 엄마는 우리를 위해 쿠키를 굽는다.

02. Mike asked ________. Mike가 내게 물었다.

03. Mina called ________. 미나가 내게 전화했다.

04. Our parents love ________. 우리 부모님은 우리를 사랑하신다.

05. My brother lends it to ________. 나의 오빠가 내게 그것을 빌려준다.

06. Dad buys ________ some colored pencils. 아빠는 우리에게 색연필 몇 자루를 사주신다.

07. Suho treats ________ differently. 수호는 나를 다르게 대한다.

08. Mr. Kim teaches ________ English. 김 선생님께서 우리에게 영어를 가르치신다.

09. Our older sister gives ________ notebooks. 우리 언니가 우리에게 공책을 준다.

10. Mom doesn't allow ________ to play. 엄마는 내가 놀지 못하게 하신다.

11. My uncle buys ________ an ice cream cake.
나의 삼촌은 내게 아이스크림 케이크를 사주신다.

12. Our children sing for ________.
우리 아이들은 우리를 위해 노래한다.

정답과 해설 p.7

Let's Practice More!

SET 05

학습목표 2 | 목적격 인칭대명사(me, you, him, her, it, us, them)를 익혀 보아요. 공부한 날 : 맞은 개수 : /14개

다음 문장의 목적격 인칭대명사 You[you]가 단수인지 복수인지 쓰세요.

01. I need you all. → 복수

02. My sons, I cannot live without you. → ________

03. Dad called you, Sihu. → ________

04. I invite all of you. → ________

05. Mom gives you a present for your birthday. → ________

06. They envy you, Mina. → ________

07. Your dad named you "Mike." → ________

08. Sorry kids, they are not for you. → ________

09. I want to share them with you, Sihu. → ________

10. I packed some cookies for you, my friends. → ________

11. We really love you, kids. → ________

12. He wants to see all of you. → ________

13. I think he likes you, Mina. → ________

14. Mom bakes cookies for you, little twins. → ________

정답과 해설 p.7

Let's Practice More!

SET 06

학습목표 2 | 목적격 인칭대명사(me, you, him, her, it, us, them)를 익혀 보아요.

공부한 날 :

맞은 개수 : /14개

다음 우리말 뜻에 맞는 인칭대명사(him, her, it, them)를 빈칸에 쓰세요.

01. They envy ___him___. 그들은 그를 부러워한다.

02. Mina wants to taste ___________. 미나는 그것을 맛보고 싶다.

03. You must share them with ___________. 넌 그녀와 그것들을 공유해야 한다.

04. Dad asked ___________. 아빠는 그들에게 물어 보셨다.

05. I will give ___________ crayons. 난 그녀에게 크레파스를 줄 것이다.

06. Mina called ___________. 미나는 그에게 전화했다.

07. Get used to ___________. 그것에 익숙해져라.

08. I hope he likes ___________. 난 그가 그것을 마음에 들어 했으면 좋겠다.

09. We eat ___________ together. 우리는 그것들을 함께 먹는다.

10. You cannot live without ___________. 넌 그녀 없이 살 수 없다.

11. Mom buys a cake for ___________. 엄마는 그를 위해 케이크를 사신다.

12. I have to share it with ___________. 난 그들과 그것을 나누어야 한다.

13. They want to eat ___________ again. 그들은 그것을 다시 먹고 싶다.

14. He invites ___________. 그는 그녀를 초대한다.

정답과 해설 p.7

Let's Practice More!

SET 07

학습목표 3 | **주격 · 목적격 인칭대명사(I, You, He, She, It, We, They, me, you, him, her, it, us, them)를 익혀요.** 공부한 날 : 맞은 개수 : /20개

다음 우리말 뜻에 맞는 인칭대명사를 빈칸에 넣어 문장을 완성해 보세요.
(I, You, He, She, It, We, They, me, you, him, her, it, us, them)

01. ____I____ asked ____him____. 난 그에게 물었다.

02. ________ loves her children. 그녀는 그녀의 아이들을 사랑한다.

03. Sihu gives ________ colored pencils. 시후는 나에게 색연필을 준다.

04. ________ draw "Meow" with ________. 나는 그것들을 가지고 '야옹이'를 그린다.

05. ________ plays mobile games. 그는 모바일 게임을 한다.

06. ________ give ________ a stuffed panda. 우리는 그녀에게 판다 인형을 준다.

07. ________ eat cookies together. 그들은 함께 쿠키를 먹는다.

08. ________ want to be like ________. 난 그녀처럼 되고 싶다.

09. The world will speak for ________. 세상이 그를 대변할 것이다.

10. ________ think ________ know everything. 그들은 그들이 모든 것을 안다고 생각한다.

11. ________ will play baseball with ________. 그는 그들과 야구를 할 것이다.

12. ________ has a fever. 그녀는 열이 있다.

13. ________ is out there. 그건 저 밖에 있어.

14. ________ bakes cookies for ________. 그녀는 우리를 위해 쿠키를 굽는다.

15. ________ is so cute. 그것은 매우 귀엽다.

16. ________ buy a present for ________. 우리는 너를 위한 선물을 산다.

17. ________ are my lovely sons. 너희들은 나의 사랑스런 아들들이다.

18. ________ don't allow ________ to play. 그들은 내가 놀지 못하게 한다.

19. ________ think ________ is not fair. 난 그것이 공평하지 않다고 생각한다.

20. ________ buys notebooks for ________. 그는 우리를 위해 공책을 산다.

정답과 해설 p.7

Let's Practice More!

SET 08

학습목표 3 | 주격 · 목적격 인칭대명사(I, You, He, She, It, We, They, me, you, him, her, it, us, them)를 익혀요.

공부한 날 :　　　맞은 개수 :　　/20개

다음 우리말 뜻에 맞는 인칭대명사를 빈칸에 넣어 문장을 완성해 보세요.
(I, You, He, She, It, We, They, me, you, him, her, it, us, them)

01. ___You___ must do ___it___ yourself. 넌 그것을 직접 해야 한다.

02. ________ made cookies for ________. 내가 너를 위해 쿠키를 만들었어.

03. ________ hope ________ likes it. 난 그가 그것을 맘에 들어 하길 바란다.

04. ________ smell delicious. 그것들은 맛있는 냄새가 난다.

05. ________ has the courage. 그녀는 용기가 있다.

06. ________ have dinner together. 그들은 함께 저녁을 먹는다.

07. Share ________ with ________. 나와 함께 그것들을 나누자.

08. ________ is turning fourteen. 그는 열네 살이 된다.

09. ________ think ________ are kind. 너는 그들이 친절하다고 생각한다.

10. ________ like ________. 우리는 그들을 좋아한다.

11. ________ think ________ is cute. 나는 그것이 귀엽다고 생각한다.

12. Does ________ watch TV? 그녀는 TV를 보니?

13. ________ bakes cookies for ________. 그는 우리를 위해 쿠키를 굽는다.

14. ________ cannot live without ________. 그들은 너 없이 살 수 없어.

15. My friends give ________ a stuffed cat. 내 친구들은 내게 고양이 인형을 준다.

16. ________ is really fluffy. 그것은 정말 보송보송하다.

17. ________ have a pajama party tonight. 우리는 오늘 밤에 파자마 파티가 있다.

18. Suho treats ________ differently. 수호는 그녀를 다르게 대한다.

19. ________ is so selfish. 그녀는 너무 이기적이다.

20. The world will speak for ________. 세상이 우리를 대변할 것이다.

정답과 해설 p.7

UNIT

03 Hayul is my little brother.

소유격 인칭대명사

❖ POiNT ❖

소유격 인칭대명사는 명사의 앞에 오고, '~의'라고 해석해요.

한 명 / 한 개 (단수)	1인칭	**my** 나의	Hayul is **my** little brother. 하율이는 나의 남동생이야.
	2인칭	**your** 너의	**Your** smartphone is amazing! 너의 스마트폰은 놀라워!
	3인칭	**his** 그의	Everybody likes **his** idea. 모든 사람들이 그의 아이디어를 좋아한다.
		her 그녀의	I love **her** voice. 나는 그녀의 목소리를 정말 좋아해.
		its 그것의	I like **its** color. 나는 그것의 색깔을 좋아해.
여러 명 / 여러 개 (복수)	1인칭	**our** 우리의	**Our** dog is so cute. 우리의 개는 매우 귀여워.
	2인칭	**your** 너희들의	We need **your** help. 우리는 너희들의 도움이 필요해.
	3인칭	**their** 그들의 그것들의	They love **their** children. 그들은 그들의 아이들을 사랑한다.

Check and Write

다음 문장을 보고 [ ]에 알맞은 소유격 인칭대명사를 쓰세요.

1. What is [your] name?
너의 이름은 무엇이니?

2. I love [ ] songs!
나는 그들의 노래들을 정말 좋아해!

3. Mom, where are [ ] socks?
엄마, 내 양말 어디 있어요?

4. Shush! That is [ ] secret.
쉿! 그것은 우리들의 비밀이야.

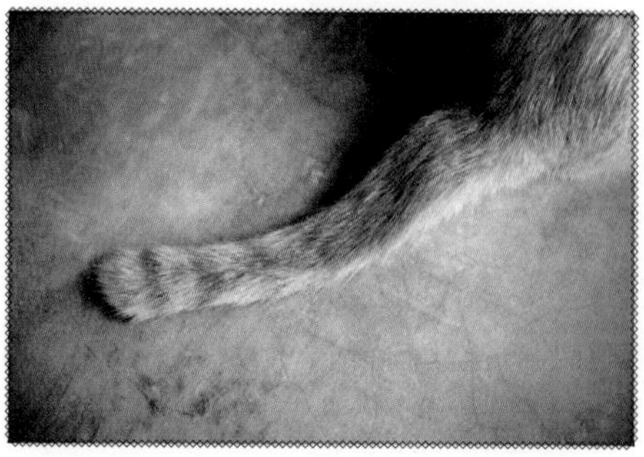

5. [ ] tail is so soft!
그것의 꼬리는 매우 부드러워!

6. I want to ride [ ] bicycle.
나는 그의 자전거를 타고 싶어요.

정답과 해설 p.7

소유대명사

UNIT 04 It is now yours.

❖ POiNT ❖

소유대명사는 '누구의 것'을 표현해요. 소유격 인칭대명사와 달리 명사의 의미까지 포함되어 있어서 뒤에 따로 명사가 오지 않아요.

한 명 / 한 개 (단수)	1인칭	**mine** 내 것	The ring is **mine**! 그 반지는 내 것이야! (= It is my ring!)
	2인칭	**yours** 너의 것	It is now **yours**. 그건 이제 너의 것이야.
	3인칭	**his** 그의 것	The broken glasses are **his**. 그 부러진 안경은 그의 것이야. 
		hers 그녀의 것	The coat in the closet is **hers**. 옷장 속에 있는 그 코트는 그녀의 것이야.

여러 명 / 여러 개 (복수)	1인칭	**ours** 우리의 것	The victory is **ours**. 승리는 우리의 것이야.
	2인칭	**yours** 너희들의 것	The choice is **yours**. 선택은 너희들의 것이야.
	3인칭	**theirs** 그들의 것	Our house is brown, and **theirs** is white. 우리 집은 갈색이고 그들의 것(집)은 흰색이야. 

Check and Write

다음 문장을 보고 [ ]에 알맞은 소유대명사를 쓰세요.

1. This toy is [mine].
이 장난감은 내 거야.

2. That one is [ ].
저게 너의 것이야.

3. This cake is for you.
이 케이크는 너를 위한 거야.
That cake is [ ].
저 케이크는 그녀의 것이야.

4. Our house is near the school.
우리 집은 학교에서 가까워.
[ ] is far from the school.
그들의 것(집)은 학교에서 멀어.

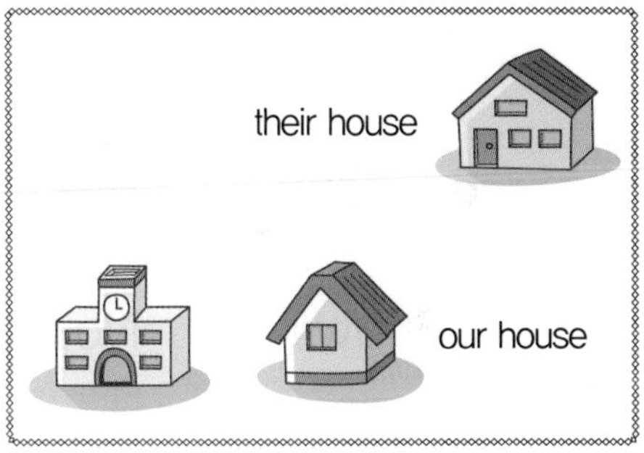

5. Whose dog is that? It is so pretty.
저것은 누구 개예요? 아주 예뻐요.
It is [ ].
그것은 너희들의 것이야.

6. Will you pass this to Sihu?
이걸 시후한테 전해줄래?
This is [ ].
이건 그의 것이야.

정답과 해설 p.8

Practice 1 소유격 인칭대명사와 소유대명사를 익혀 보아요.

다음 문장에 알맞은 인칭대명사를 보기 에서 골라 빈칸 안에 써 보세요. (단, 한 번 쓴 말은 또 쓸 수 있어요.)

A In the locker room

보기 my[My] your[Your] mine[Mine] yours[Yours]

1. *Mina* : Take off ___your___ shoes. They are dirty.
네 신발을 벗어. 그것들은 더러워.

2. *Yuri* : __________ are dirty, too! 네 것들도 더러워!

3. *Mina* : Is this swimsuit __________? 이 수영복 네 것이니?

4. *Yuri* : No. That is not __________. 아니. 그건 내 것이 아냐.

5. *Mina* : Did you see __________ swimming goggles?
너 나의 물안경 봤니?

6. *Yuri* : Are those __________ on the bench? 벤치 위에 있는 저것들이 네 거야?

7. *Mina* : No. I think my sister took __________.
아니. 내 생각에 우리 언니가 내 것을 가져간 거 같아.

B Back-to-school shopping

보기 my[My] his[His] its[Its]

1. Sihu, __________ little brother, went shopping. 내 남동생 시후는 쇼핑을 갔다.

2. He was excited to buy __________ new notebooks.
그는 그의 새 공책들을 사는 것에 신이 나 있었다.

3. Last year, __________ notebooks were wide ruled.
작년에 그의 공책들은 줄 간격이 넓었다. (*wide ruled: 줄 간격이 넓은)

정답과 해설 p.8

4. Now, __________ new notebooks are college ruled.
이제, 그의 새 공책들은 줄 간격이 좁다. **(*college ruled: 줄 간격이 좁은)**

5. He bought a pen. __________ cap has a cute character on it.
그는 펜 한 자루를 샀다. 그것의 뚜껑에는 귀여운 캐릭터가 있다.

CH 03

C I got a haircut.

보기 his her hers

1. Mina had __________ hair cut today. 미나는 오늘 그녀의 머리카락을 잘랐다.

2. The hairdresser said that it was __________ first day.
미용사는 그의(그가 일하는) 첫날이라고 말했다.

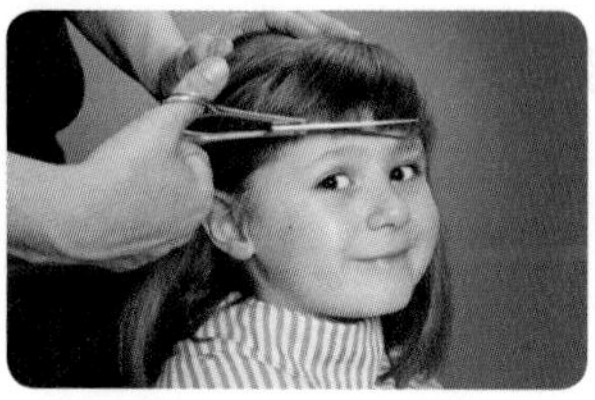

3. He cut __________ hair shorter than she asked.
그는 그녀의 머리를 그녀가 요구한 것보다 더 짧게 잘랐다.

4. Boys have longer hair than __________!
남자애들이 그녀의 것보다 더 긴 머리카락을 갖고 있어!

D Attention, please!

보기 our your

1. May I have __________ attention, please?
여러분 주목해주시겠습니까?

2. Welcome aboard __________ camp bus.
저희 캠프 버스에 타신 것을 환영합니다.

3. Please fasten __________ seatbelt for __________ safety.
여러분의 안전을 위해 여러분의 안전벨트를 착용해 주세요.

4. If you have any questions, please ask one of __________ staff.
문의사항이 있으면, 우리 직원들 중 한 명에게 물어보세요.

정답과 해설 p.8

Practice 2 소유격 인칭대명사와 소유대명사를 문장으로 익혀보아요.

다음 우리말 뜻과 같도록 빈칸에 알맞은 단어를 넣어 문장을 완성하세요.

1. Did you see ___my___ eraser? 너 내 지우개 봤니?

2. Sihu had __________ hair cut today. 시후는 오늘 그의 머리를 잘랐다.

3. Can I use __________ phone? 내가 네 전화기를 써도 되겠니?

4. Sure. Where is __________? 물론이지. 네 것은 어디 있니?

5. __________ is broken. 내 것은 고장났어.

6. The hairdresser cut __________ hair too short. 미용사가 그의 머리를 너무 짧게 잘랐다.

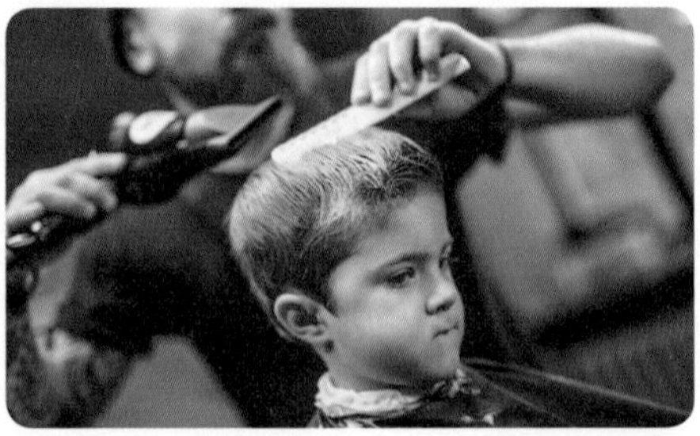

7. No, it's Mina's. I think __________ brother took mine. 아니, 그건 미나 거야. 내 생각에 내 남동생이 내 걸 가져간 것 같아.

정답과 해설 p.8

8. Isn't that ___________? 저거 네 거 아냐?

9. It is __________ pleasure to meet you. 저희는 여러분을 만나게 되어 기쁩니다.

10. Enjoy ___________ flight.
여러분의 비행을 즐기세요(즐거운 비행 되세요).

11. Please fasten ___________ seatbelt.
여러분의 안전벨트를 매 주시기 바랍니다.

12. We ask that trays be in ___________ full upright position.
선반들을 완전히 올려주시기를 요청합니다.

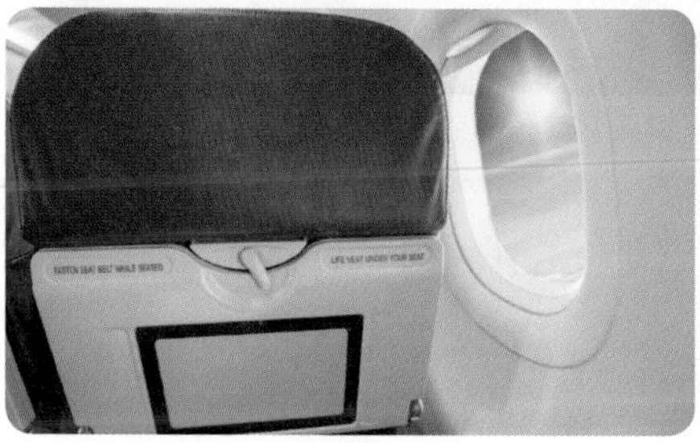

13. I don't like ___________ new haircut. 나는 내 새로운 머리 모양이 마음에 들지 않아.

14. She is talking in ___________ sleep. 그녀는 자면서 말하고 있어(잠꼬대를 하고 있어).

15. Love is putting someone else's needs before ___________.
사랑이란 다른 누군가의 욕구를 네 것보다 앞에 놓는 거야(우선시하는 거야).

정답과 해설 p.8

16. __________ choices make us. 우리의 선택들이 우리를 만든다.

17. She is __________ sister. 그녀는 나의 누나야.

18. The book is __________. 그 책은 그녀의 것이야.

19. We both like __________ coach, Joe.
우리는 둘 다 우리의 코치인 Joe를 좋아한다.

20. She reads a book in __________ room.
그녀는 그녀의 방에서 책을 읽는다.

Cultural Tips
재미로 익히는 문화상식

영어로 이름 나타내기!

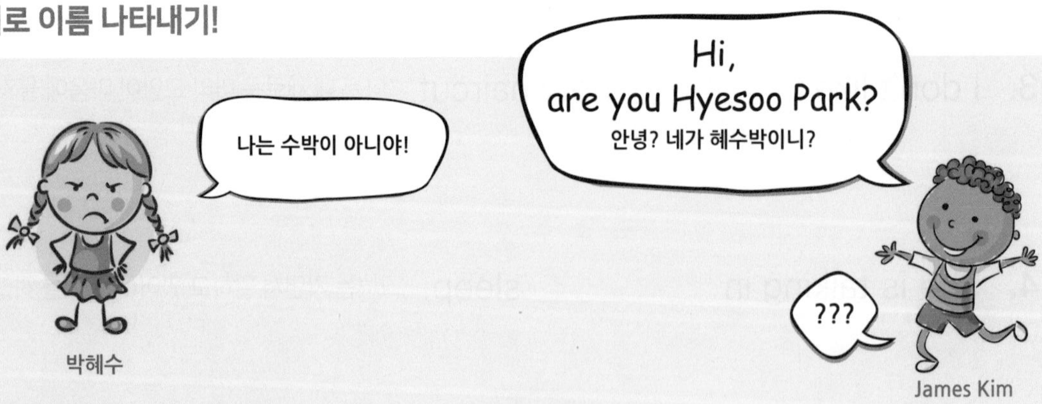

아이쿠, 저런! 혜수가 오해를 했네요!
우리나라에서는 이름을 표현할 때, 성(박)이 먼저 오고 그 다음에 이름(혜수)이 오죠?
하지만 미국에서는 이름(James)이 먼저 오고, 성(Kim)이 뒤에 온답니다.
그래서 영어에서는 이름을 'first name'이라고 하고, 성을 'last name'이라고 해요.
박혜수는 당연히 Hyesoo Park이라고 표현하겠죠?

정답과 해설 p.8

Practice 3 소유격 인칭대명사와 소유대명사를 사용하여 문장을 완성해 보아요.

다음 우리말 뜻과 같도록 주어진 표현을 순서에 맞게 배열하여 문장을 완성해 보세요.

1. Excuse me. I think (seat, you are in, my).
실례합니다. 제 생각에 당신이 제 자리에 앉은 것 같아요.
→ Excuse me. I think ___you are in my seat___.

2. Let me (ticket, check, my). 제 표를 확인해 볼게요.
→ Let me ______________.

3. (is 7B, seat number, My), car 5. 제 좌석 번호는 5호차의 7B예요.
→ ______________, car 5.

4. But (car number, is, your) 6. 그런데 당신의 열차 번호는 6호차예요.
→ But ______________ 6.

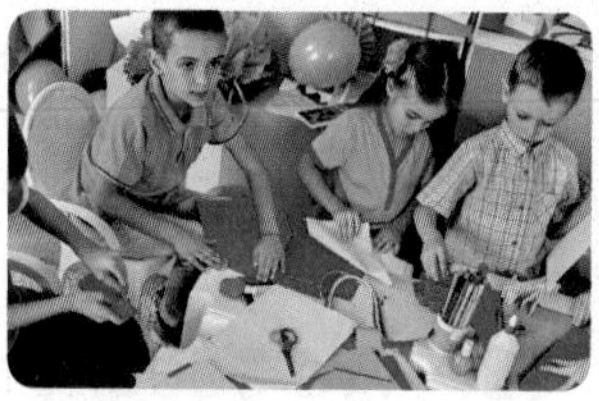

5. Can I (scissors, borrow, your)? 내가 네 가위를 빌릴 수 있을까?
→ Can I ______________?

6. Sure. (yours, What's wrong, with)?
물론이지. 네 것은 뭔가 잘못됐니?
→ Sure. ______________?

7. (mine, took, brother, My). He lost his.
내 형이 내 것을 가져갔어. 그가 그의 것을 잃어버렸거든.
→ ______________. He lost his.

8. You got a haircut! I really (new look, your, like).
너 머리 잘랐구나! 난 네 새 모습이 정말 마음에 든다.
→ You got a haircut! I really ______________.

정답과 해설 p.8

9. Do you? I was worried that (my, too short, cut it, hairdresser).
그래? 난 내 미용사가 너무 짧게 잘라서 걱정했는데.

➔ Do you? I was worried that ______________________________.

10. (is, mine, It, better than). I need to do something with my hair.
그건 내 것보다 나아. 난 내 머리를 어떻게 좀 해야겠어.

➔ ______________________________. I need to do something with my hair.

11. (and I, My, went shopping, sister). 내 여동생과 나는 쇼핑을 갔다.

➔ ______________________________.

12. She was excited to (shopping list, her, check).
그녀는 그녀의 쇼핑 목록을 확인하며 신이 났다.

➔ She was excited to ______________________________.

13. We bought two rulers. She (Hello Kitty ruler, liked, her).
우리는 자를 두 개 샀다. 그녀는 그녀의 헬로 키티 자를 마음에 들어했다.

➔ We bought two rulers. She ______________________________.

14. My ruler doesn't have Kitty on it, but (longer than, mine, hers, is).
내 자에는 키티가 없지만 내 것이 그녀의 것보다 길다.

➔ My ruler doesn't have Kitty on it, but ______________________________.

15. I bought her an eraser because (mine, always borrows, she).
나는 그녀에게 지우개를 하나 사줬는데 왜냐하면 그녀는 항상 내 것을 빌려가기 때문이다.

➔ I bought her an eraser because ______________________________.

정답과 해설 p.8

16. We also (notebooks, our, bought).
우리는 우리의 공책들도 샀다.

➔ We also ______________________.

17. Her notebooks (mine, are different from).
그녀의 공책들은 내 것과 다르다.

➔ Her notebooks ______________________.

18. I was (room, in, his, taking a nap). 나는 그의 방에서 낮잠을 자는 중이었다.

➔ I was ______________________.

19. Love is putting (yours, before, someone else's needs).
사랑이란 다른 누군가의 욕구를 네 것보다 앞에 놓는 것이다(우선시하는 것이다).

➔ Love is putting ______________________.

20. (teacher, teaches math, Their). 그들의 선생님은 수학을 가르치신다.

➔ ______________________.

※인칭대명사를 표로 한눈에 정리해 보아요.

		주격	소유격	목적격	소유대명사
단수	1인칭	I	my	me	mine
	2인칭	you	your	you	yours
	3인칭	she	her	her	hers
		he	his	him	his
		it	its	it	-
복수	1인칭	we	our	us	ours
	2인칭	you	your	you	yours
	3인칭	they	their	them	theirs

정답과 해설 p.8

Let's Practice More!

SET 01

학습목표 1 | **소유격 인칭대명사(my, your, his, her, its, our, their)를 익혀보아요.**

공부한 날 :　　　　맞은 개수 :　　　/12개

( ) 안에 주어진 대명사를 알맞은 소유격 인칭대명사 형태로 바꿔 빈칸에 쓰세요.

01. Please fasten ___your___ seatbelt. (you)
안전벨트를 매 주세요.

02. Welcome aboard __________ camp bus. (we)
우리의 캠프 버스에 탑승하신 것을 환영해요.

03. They take __________ goggles. (we) 그들은 우리의 고글을 가져간다.

04. I love __________ songs! (they) 나는 그들의 노래를 아주 좋아해!

05. Enjoy __________ flight. (you) 여러분의 비행을 즐기세요(즐거운 비행 되세요).

06. They love __________ children. (they) 그들은 그들의 아이들을 사랑한다.

07. __________ car number is 6. (I) 내 차량 번호는 6이다.

08. __________ choices make us. (we) 우리의 선택이 우리를 만든다.

09. Did you see __________ eraser? (she) 그녀의 지우개를 보았니?

10. Can I use __________ phone? (she) 내가 그녀의 휴대폰을 사용할 수 있니?

11. We talk about __________ test. (we) 우리는 우리의 시험에 대해 이야기한다.

12. She reads a book in __________ room. (she) 그녀는 그녀의 방에서 책을 읽는다.

정답과 해설 p.8

Let's Practice More!

SET 02

학습목표 1 | 소유격 인칭대명사(my, your, his, her, its, our, their)를 익혀보아요.

공부한 날 :　　　맞은 개수 :　　　/14개

다음 (　) 안에서 알맞은 것을 고르세요.

01. Did you see (my / mine) goggles? 너는 내 고글을 보았니?

02. May I have (yours / your) attention, please? 주목해주시겠어요?

03. The hairdresser cut (him / his) hair too short. 미용사는 그의 머리를 너무 짧게 잘랐어.

04. She buys (her / hers) new notebooks. 그녀는 그녀의 새 공책들을 사.

05. Can I borrow (you / your) scissors? 내가 너의 가위를 빌릴 수 있을까?

06. We both like (our / ours) coach, Joe. 우리는 둘 다 우리의 코치 Joe를 좋아한다.

07. (My / Mine) brother went shopping. 내 남동생은 쇼핑하러 갔다.

08. They feel that it is (their / theirs) duty. 그들은 그것이 그들의 의무라고 느낀다.

09. I sleep in (he / his) room. 나는 그의 방에서 잔다.

10. Please fasten (you / your) seat belt. 안전벨트를 매 주세요.

11. I like (her / hers) new look. 나는 그녀의 새로운 모습이 좋아.

12. Today is (theirs / their) first day. 오늘은 그들의 첫날이다.

13. Let me check (you / your) ticket. 당신의 표 좀 확인할게요.

14. (They / Their) teacher teaches math. 그들의 선생님은 수학을 가르치셔.

정답과 해설 p.8

Let's Practice More!

SET 03

학습목표 1 | **소유격 인칭대명사(my, your, his, her, its, our, their)를 익혀보아요.** 공부한 날 : 맞은 개수 : /14개

다음 우리말 뜻에 맞는 소유격 인칭대명사(my, your, his, her, its, our, their)를 빈칸에 넣어 보세요.

01. ____His____ notebooks are wide ruled.
그의 공책들은 줄 간격이 넓다.

02. He also buys __________ notebooks.
그는 그녀의 공책들도 산다.

03. __________ choices make us. 우리의 선택들이 우리를 만든다.

04. __________ seat number is 7B, car 5. 당신의 좌석 번호는 5호차의 7B예요.

05. You are in __________ seat. 당신이 제 자리에 앉아 있어요.

06. Let me check __________ ticket. 제 표를 확인해 볼게요.

07. I don't like __________ new haircut. 나는 나의 새 머리 모양이 마음에 들지 않아.

08. __________ notebooks are college ruled. 너의 공책들은 줄 간격이 좁다.

09. __________ cap has a cute character on it. 그것의 뚜껑에는 귀여운 캐릭터가 있다.

10. I had __________ hair cut today. 나는 오늘 나의 머리카락을 잘랐다.

11. She checks __________ shopping list.
그녀는 그녀의 쇼핑 목록을 확인한다.

12. He likes __________ Mickey Mouse ruler. 그는 그의 미키마우스 자를 좋아한다.

13. Please ask one of __________ staff. 우리 직원들 중 한 명에게 물어보세요.

14. He and __________ friend went shopping. 그와 그의 친구는 쇼핑을 하러 갔다.

정답과 해설 p.8

Let's Practice More!

SET 04

학습목표 2 | 소유대명사(mine, yours, his, hers, ours, theirs)를 익혀보아요. 공부한 날 : 맞은 개수 : /12개

( ) 안에 주어진 대명사를 알맞은 소유대명사 형태로 바꿔 빈칸에 쓰세요.

01. This book is mine. (I)
이 책은 나의 것이야.

02. The broken glasses are __________.
(he) 그 부러진 안경은 그의 것이야.

03. That is not __________. (you) 저것은 너의 것이 아니야.

04. Her reality is different from __________. (we) 그녀의 현실은 우리의 것과 달라.

05. She always borrows __________. (he) 그녀는 항상 그의 것을 빌려.

06. The coat is __________. (me) 그 코트는 내 것이야.

07. He lost __________. (he) 그는 그의 것을 잃어버렸다.

08. It is better than __________. (they) 그것은 그들의 것보다 낫다.

09. __________ are pretty, too. (we) 우리의 것도 예쁘다.

10. __________ was broken. (she) 그녀의 것은 부러졌어.

11. Mine is shorter than __________. (he) 나의 것은 그의 것보다 짧아.

12. __________ are on the table. (they) 그들의 것은 테이블 위에 있어.

정답과 해설 p.8

Let's Practice More!

SET 05

학습목표 2 | 소유대명사(mine, yours, his, hers, ours, theirs)를 익혀보아요. 공부한 날 : 맞은 개수 : /14개

다음 ( ) 안에서 알맞은 것을 고르세요.

01. It is better than (my / mine). 그것은 내 것보다 나아.

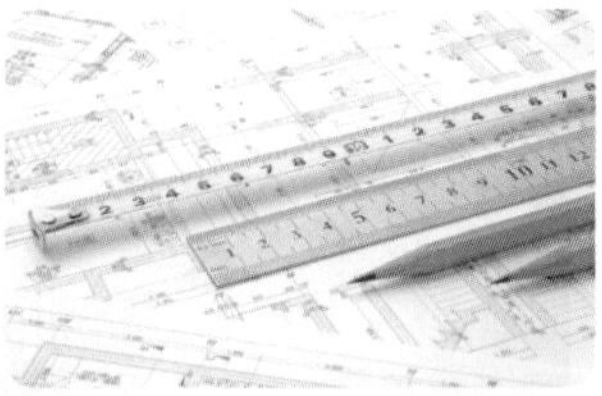

02. Mine is longer than (hers / her). 내 것은 그녀의 것보다 더 길어.

03. She always borrows (mine / my). 그녀는 항상 내 것을 빌려.

04. Are those (he / his) on the desk? 책상 위에 있는 그것들은 그의 것이니?

05. That cake is (our / ours). 저 케이크는 우리의 것이야.

06. Her notebooks are different from (I / mine).
그녀의 공책들은 나의 것과 다르다.

07. The ring is (yours / your). 그 반지는 너의 것이다.

08. Is this swimsuit (her / hers)? 이 수영복이 그녀의 것이니?

09. Where is (my / mine)? 나의 것이 어디 있니?

10. Your house is near the school. (Our / Ours) is far from the school.
너의 집은 학교와 가까워. 우리의 것(집)은 학교에서 멀어.

11. (Yours / Your) are dirty. 너의 것은 더럽다.

12. My brother took mine. He lost (him / his).
나의 남동생이 나의 것을 가져갔어. 그는 그의 것을 잃어버렸어.

13. Our house is brown, and (hers / her) is white.
우리의 집은 갈색이고 그녀의 것(집)은 하얀색이다.

14. What's wrong with (your / yours)? 너의 것에 무슨 문제가 있니?

정답과 해설 p.8

Let's Practice More!

SET 06

학습목표 2 | **소유대명사(mine, yours, his, hers, ours, theirs)를 익혀보아요.** 공부한 날 : 맞은 개수 : /14개

다음 우리말 뜻에 맞는 소유대명사(mine, yours, his, hers, ours, theirs)를 빈칸에 쓰세요.

01. The coat is ___his___.
그 코트는 그의 것이야.

02. The ring is __________.
그 반지는 그녀의 것이야.

03. My reality is different from __________. 내 현실은 그녀의 것과 다르다.

04. That is not __________. 저건 네 것이 아냐.

05. __________ was broken. 네 것은 고장 났어.

06. Love is putting someone else's needs before __________.
사랑은 다른 누군가의 욕구를 네 것보다 앞에 놓는 거야(우선시하는 거야).

07. That cake is __________. 저 케이크는 우리의 것이야.

08. Is this swimsuit __________? 이 수영복은 그녀의 것이니?

09. This house is __________. 이 집은 우리의 것(집)이야.

10. __________ are on the table. 그들의 것은 테이블 위에 있어.

11. __________ are dirty, too. 네 것들도 더러워.

12. Are those __________ on the bench? 벤치에 있는 저것들이 그의 것이야?

13. She lost __________. 그녀는 그녀의 것을 잃어버렸다.

14. Our house is red, and __________ is white. 우리 집은 빨간색이고 그들의 것(집)은 흰색이야.

정답과 해설 p.8

Let's Practice More!

SET 07

학습목표 3 | **소유격 인칭대명사와 소유대명사를 비교해 보아요.** 공부한 날 : 맞은 개수 : /20개

보기와 같이 밑줄 친 부분이 소유격 인칭대명사면 A를, 소유대명사면 B를 괄호 안에 쓰세요.

보기 That is my ball. (A) The new shoes are mine. (B)

01. He lost his watch. (A)
그는 그의 시계를 잃어버렸어.

02. I like her new cap. ( )
나는 그녀의 새로운 모자가 좋아.

03. He borrows my pen. 그는 나의 펜을 빌린다. ( )

04. Please fasten your seatbelt. 안전벨트를 매 주세요. ( )

05. The socks are yours. 그 양말은 너의 것이야. ( )

06. I love his pictures! 나는 그의 그림이 매우 좋아! ( )

07. Is this earring hers? 이 귀걸이가 그녀의 것이니? ( )

08. Mom takes my goggles. 엄마는 내 고글을 가져가신다. ( )

09. Can I use your ruler? 내가 너의 자를 사용할 수 있을까? ( )

정답과 해설 p.8

10. Her car is different from mine. 그녀의 차는 내 것과 다르다. ( )

11. I check my schedule. 나는 내 일정을 확인한다. ( )

12. Are those theirs on the desk? 책상 위에 있는 저것들은 그들의 것이니? ( )

13. He reads a book in his classroom. 그는 그의 교실에서 책을 읽는다. ( )

14. That chocolate is mine. 저 초콜릿은 나의 것이야. ( )

15. They love their dogs. 그들은 그들의 개를 아주 좋아한다. ( )

16. Welcome aboard our camp bus. 우리의 캠프 버스에 탑승하신 것을 환영해요. ( )

17. My car is red, and his is black. 내 차는 빨간색이고 그의 것은 검은색이다. ( )

18. He and his friend went to the movie. ( )
그와 그의 친구는 영화를 보러 갔다.

19. Your seat number is 6A. 너의 좌석 번호는 6A이다. ( )

20. Our choices make us. 우리의 선택이 우리를 만든다. ( )

정답과 해설 p.8

Let's Practice More!

SET 08

학습목표 3 | **소유격 인칭대명사와 소유대명사를 비교해 보아요.** 공부한 날 : 맞은 개수 : /20개

다음 우리말 뜻과 같도록 빈칸에 알맞은 단어를 넣어 문장을 완성하세요.

01. He borrows ___her___ pencil.
그는 그녀의 연필을 빌린다.

02. Can I borrow __________ __________?
내가 네 가위를 빌릴 수 있을까?

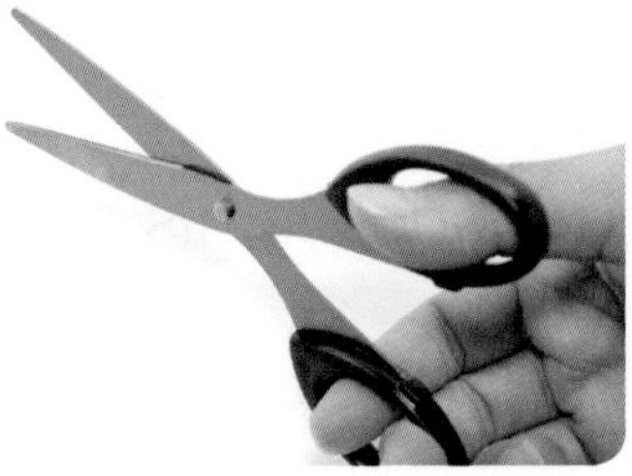

03. __________ __________ are wide ruled. 그의 공책들은 줄 간격이 넓다.

04. It is better than __________. 그건 그들의 것보다 낫다.

05. I think you are in __________ __________. 제 생각에 당신이 제 자리에 앉은 것 같아요.

06. __________ seat is not here. 당신의 자리는 여기가 아닙니다.

07. The ring is __________. 그 반지는 그녀의 것이야.

08. Mine is shorter than __________. 내 것이 그의 것보다 짧다.

09. Please ask one of __________ staff. 우리 직원들 중 한 명에게 물어보세요.

정답과 해설 p.8

10. I don't like ________ ________ ________. 나는 내 새로운 머리 모양이 마음에 들지 않아.

11. Are those ________ on the roof? 지붕 위에 있는 저것들이 우리의 것이야?

12. My house is red, and ________ is white. 나의 집은 빨간색이고 그녀의 것(집)은 흰색이야.

CH 03

13. ________ ________ ________ is 7B, car 5. 당신의 좌석 번호는 5호차의 7B예요.

14. It is ________ pleasure to meet you. 저희는 여러분을 만나게 되어 기쁩니다.

15. It is not ________.
그건 네 것이 아냐.

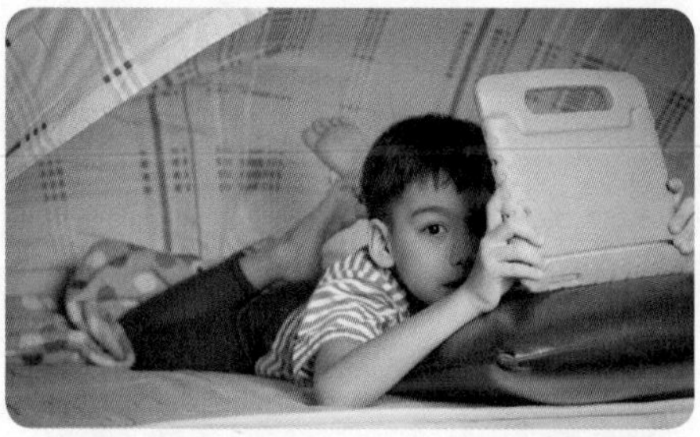

16. ________ flowers are pretty.
너의 꽃들은 예뻐.

17. ________ choices make us. 우리의 선택들이 우리를 만든다.

18. ________ are dirty. 네 것들은 더러워.

19. ________ are on the table. 그들의 것은 테이블 위에 있어.

20. Sihu had ________ ________ cut today. 시후는 오늘 그의 머리를 잘랐다.

정답과 해설 p.8

Chapter 04 지시대명사와 비인칭주어 it

이 챕터에서는 무엇인가를 가리킬 때 대신 쓰는 명사(대명사)인 '지시대명사'와 시간, 날짜, 요일, 날씨, 계절, 거리, 명암 등을 나타낼 때 쓰는 비인칭주어 'it'에 대해 배워 봐요.

☆ 학습 방향 및 배울 내용 미리보기 ☆

☐ **Unit 01 : That** is my uncle.

지시대명사 this, these / that, those / it

지시대명사는 어느 때 쓰고, 어떤 것이 있는지 배워 봐요.

▼

☐ **Unit 02 : It** is 9 o'clock. I'm late for school!

지시형용사 / 비인칭주어 it

지시형용사가 무엇인지, 그리고 비인칭주어는 언제 쓰는지 배워 봐요.

단어 미리보기

이 챕터에 나올 단어들 중 이미 알고 있는 단어가 있나요?
맞는 뜻을 골라 체크해 봐요.

날짜 : 이름 : 알고 있는 단어의 수 : /24개

No.	아는 단어	단어	품사	알맞은 뜻에 체크 표시해 봐요.			
1	☑	strong	형용사	강한	☑	약한	☐
2	☐	uncle	명사	이모	☐	삼촌	☐
3	☐	toy	명사	장난감	☐	로봇	☐
4	☐	gun	명사	껌	☐	총	☐
5	☐	doughnut	명사	도넛	☐	땅콩	☐
6	☐	candy	명사	설탕	☐	사탕	☐
7	☐	egg	명사	계란	☐	병아리	☐
8	☐	run	동사	달리다	☐	걷다	☐
9	☐	snowy	형용사	비 내리는	☐	눈 내리는	☐
10	☐	light	명사	전등	☐	의자	☐
11	☐	play	동사	싸우다	☐	놀다	☐
12	☐	cookie	명사	쿠키	☐	초콜릿	☐
13	☐	winter	명사	가을	☐	겨울	☐
14	☐	already	부사	이미	☐	나중에	☐
15	☐	star	명사	별	☐	달	☐
16	☐	year	명사	해(년)	☐	일	☐
17	☐	weekend	명사	주말	☐	주중	☐
18	☐	often	부사	가끔	☐	자주	☐
19	☐	photo	명사	사진	☐	낙서	☐
20	☐	real	형용사	가짜의	☐	진짜의	☐
21	☐	grandfather	명사	할머니	☐	할아버지	☐
22	☐	bad	형용사	나쁜	☐	좋은	☐
23	☐	diary	명사	이야기	☐	일기장	☐
24	☐	sad	형용사	슬픈	☐	화난	☐

UNIT

01 That is my uncle.

지시대명사 this, these / that, those / it

지시대명사는 무엇인가를 가리킬(지시할) 때 대신 쓰는 명사(대명사)로 수와 거리에 따라 다르게 사용해요.

❖ POiNT 1 ❖

가까운 것을 가리키는 this, these

This is my pet.
이것은 내 애완동물이다.

This is Yechan.
이 사람은 예찬이야.

These are strong mice.
이것들은 힘 센 쥐들이다.

These are my friends.
이 사람들은 내 친구들이야.

❖ POiNT 2 ❖

먼 것을 가리키는 that, those

That is an ugly rat.
저것은 못생긴 쥐이다.

That is my uncle.
저 사람은 내 삼촌이야.

I'm not afraid of those.
나는 저것들이 무섭지 않아.

Those are my cousins.
저 사람들은 나의 사촌들이야.

❖ POiNT 3 ❖

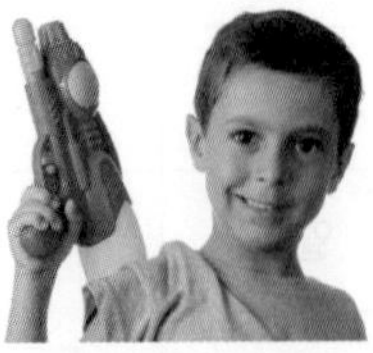

앞에 나온 내용이나 단어를 가리키는 it

You got a new toy gun. I like it.
너는 새로운 장난감 총을 받았구나. 난 그것(장난감 총)이 좋아.

Check and Write

다음 우리말 해석을 참고하여 [   ]에 알맞은 말을 쓰세요.

1. [These] are my friends.

이 사람들은 내 친구들이야.

2. I got a Nintendo. I love [   ].

나는 닌텐도를 받았어. 나는 그것이 아주 마음에 들어.

3. [   ] is our house.

이것은 우리 집이야.

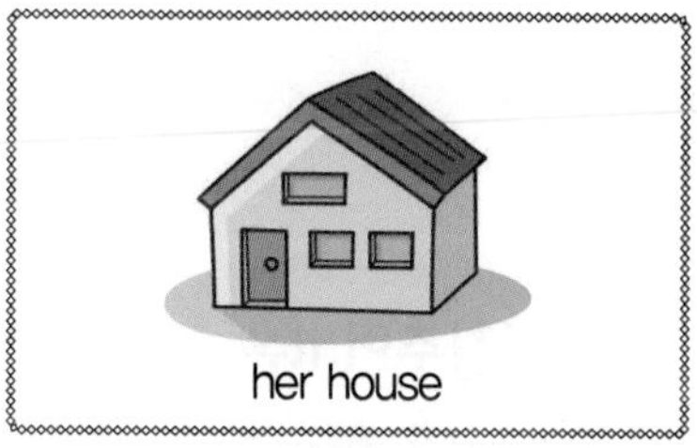

4. [   ] is her house.

저것은 그녀의 집이야.

5. Whose doughnuts are [   ]?

이것들은 누구의 도넛들이에요?

6. [   ] are Mina's candies.

저것들은 미나의 사탕이야.

7. When did you buy your new kick scooter?

I love [   ]!

너는 너의 새로운 킥보드를 언제 샀어? 나 그거 아주 마음에 들어!

정답과 해설 p.9

UNIT 02 It is 9 o'clock. I'm late for school!

지시형용사 / 비인칭주어 it

❖ POiNT 1 ❖

지시형용사는 위치의 정보를 주면서 명사를 꾸며줄 수 있어요.

Yejin: I'm hungry. Can I have this cake?

저 배고파요. 이 케이크 먹어도 돼요?

Mom: Sorry, but the cake is for your dad.

미안하지만 그 케이크는 너의 아빠를 위한 거야.

Junwoo: Let's take these eggs home.

우리 이 알들을 집에 가져가자.

Sihu: Maybe those crocodiles are their parents! Run!

아마 저 악어들이 그것들의 부모인가 봐! 도망쳐!

❖ POiNT 2 ❖

비인칭주어 it은 시간, 날짜, 요일, 날씨, 계절, 거리, 명암 등을 나타낼 때 쓰고 이때 it은 해석하지 않아요.

시간

It is 9 o'clock.
I'm late for school!

9시 정각이야. 난 학교에 늦었어!

날짜 / 요일

It is December 25th. 12월 25일이야.

It is Monday. 월요일이야.

날씨

It is snowy. Let's have a snowball fight!

눈이 와. 우리 눈싸움하자!

계절

It is spring now.

지금은 봄이야.

거리

It is far from my home to school.

우리 집에서 학교까지는 멀어.

명암

It is dark in here. Turn on the light.

여기 어두워. 불 좀 켜봐.

Check and Write

다음 우리말 해석을 참고하여 [ ]에 알맞은 말을 쓰세요.

1. [It] is rainy. We can't play outside.
비가 와. 우리는 밖에서 놀 수 없어.

2. [ ] cookies are yummy.
이 쿠키들은 맛있어.

3. Why are you wearing a winter jacket?
[ ] is spring now.
너 왜 겨울 재킷을 입고 있니? 지금 봄이야.

4. Hurry up! [ ] is already 2 p.m.
서둘러! 벌써 오후 2시야.

5. Look at [ ] dog! 저 개를 봐!

6. Maybe [ ] children are its owners.
아마 저 아이들이 그것의 주인인가 봐.

7. No way! [ ] is Monday!
We have to go to school.
말도 안 돼! 월요일이야! 우린 학교에 가야 해.

정답과 해설 p.9

Practice 1 상황에 맞는 지시대명사, 지시형용사, it의 쓰임을 익혀 보아요.

다음 문장에 알맞은 말을 보기 에서 골라 빈칸에 쓰세요. (단, 한 번 쓴 말은 또 쓸 수 있어요.)

A In the planetarium

보기 that[That] those it[It]

1. I went to the planetarium. ____It____ was an amazing place.
   나는 천문관에 갔다. 그것은 놀라운 곳이었다. (*planetarium: 천문관)

2. __________ was dark inside. 안쪽은 어두웠다.

3. __________ showed me the night sky.
   그것은 내게 밤하늘을 보여주었다.

4. __________ made my jaw drop. 저것은 내 입을 떡 벌어지게 했다.

5. All __________ stars were shining. 그 모든 별들이 빛나고 있었다.

6. I didn't know that there were so many stars like __________.
   나는 별들이 저렇게 많은 줄 몰랐다.

7. I found the Milky Way. I hadn't seen __________ before. (*Milky Way: 은하수)
   나는 은하수를 발견했다. 나는 전에 그걸 본 적이 없었다.

8. __________ was wonderful. 그건 굉장히 멋졌다.

9. Why can't I see __________ stars? 왜 그 별들을 볼 수 없는 걸까?

B I found a photo.

보기 that[That] this

1. *Sihu* : Who is __________ in __________ photo?
   이 사진 속의 이분은 누구예요?

정답과 해설 p.9

2. *Dad* : ___________ is your grandfather. Where did you find the photo?
그분은 네 할아버지야. 그 사진은 어디에서 찾았니?

3. *Sihu* : It was in ___________ book.
저 책 안에 있었어요.

C White Christmas

보기 this it[It]

1. Christmas is on Friday ___________ year.
올해 크리스마스는 금요일이다.

2. ___________ is a three-day weekend!
3일 연휴다!

3. ___________ would be a white Christmas.
화이트 크리스마스가 될 거야(크리스마스에 눈이 올 거야).

4. But, ___________ doesn't snow that often in Busan.
하지만 부산에는 눈이 그렇게 자주 오지 않아.

D What day is it today?

[1~4] 다음 빈칸에 알맞은 단어를 넣어 문장을 완성하세요.

1. What day is ___________ today? 오늘 무슨 요일이야?

2. ___________ is Thursday. 목요일이야.

3. Is ___________ rainy? 비가 오니?

4. No, ___________ is snowing. 아니, 눈이 오고 있어.

정답과 해설 p.9

Practice 2 지시대명사, 지시형용사, 비인칭주어 it이 들어간 문장을 완성해 보아요.

다음 우리말 뜻과 같도록 주어진 표현을 순서에 맞게 배열하여 문장을 완성하세요.

1. (all, Look at, these stars)! 이 모든 별들을 봐!

➔ Look at all these stars !

2. What is (star, that, the name of)? 저 별 이름이 뭐예요?

➔ What is ____________________?

3. (It, bright, is, so). 그건 정말 밝아요.

➔ ____________________.

4. (is called, That, Sirius). 저것은 시리우스라고 불려.

➔ ____________________.

5. (a, is, bright star, It). 그것은 밝은 별이야.

➔ ____________________.

6. (Christmas Eve, It, is). 크리스마스이브다.

➔ ____________________.

7. (is, It, six thirty). 여섯 시 삼십 분이다.

➔ ____________________.

8. (dark, It, already, is). 벌써 어둡다.

➔ ____________________.

9. (books, These, mine, are). 이 책들은 내 것이다.

➔ ____________________.

10. (would be, a white Christmas, It). 화이트 크리스마스가 될 거야(크리스마스에 눈이 올 거야).

➔ ____________________.

정답과 해설 p.9

11. (snow, Let, it)!

눈이 내리게 해 주세요!

➔ ______________________!

12. (snowed, It, yesterday).

어제는 눈이 내렸다.

➔ ______________________.

13. (cloudy, is, It). 날씨가 흐리다.

➔ ____.

14. Did you make (things, these, all)? 이 모든 것들을 네가 만들었니?

➔ Did you make ______________________________?

15. (it, rains, When), you put on a coat. 비가 오면 너는 코트를 걸치지.

➔ ______________________, you put on a coat.

16. (is, This, the real world)! 이건 실제 세상이야!

➔ ____!

17. (It, dark and rainy, is). 어둡고 비가 내리고 있다.

➔ ____.

18. (thing, another, That's) we have in common.

그게 우리가 가진 또 다른 공통점이네.

➔ ______________________ we have in common.

19. (That's, a, choice, bad). 그것은 나쁜 선택이다.

➔ ____.

20. (is, It, too late). 너무 늦었어.

➔ ____.

CH 04

Practice 3 지시대명사, 지시형용사, it을 써서 완전한 문장을 써 보아요.

다음 우리말 뜻과 같도록 주어진 표현을 사용하여 문장을 완성하세요.

1. 이 책은 어떤 내용이에요? (What is, about)
➔ What is this book about ?

2. 그건 낡아 보여요. (looks, old)
➔ ______________________________.

3. 저건 네 아버지의 일기장이야. (father's diary)
➔ ______________________________.

4. 그것을 어디에서 찾았니? (Where did you find)
➔ ______________________________?

5. 저 책들 사이에 있었어요. (was, between)
➔ ______________________________.

6. 몇 시예요? (What, time)
➔ ______________________________?

7. 일곱 시 정각이야. (7 o'clock)
➔ ______________________________.

8. 오늘 추워요? (cold, today)
➔ ______________________________?

9. 춥고 바람이 불어. (cold and windy)
➔ ______________________________.

10. 나는 이번 크리스마스에 눈이 오길 바란다. (snows, this Christmas)
➔ I hope ______________________________.

정답과 해설 p.9

11. 오늘은 12월 25일이고, 날씨가 맑다. (sunny)

➜ Today is December 25th and ______________________.

12. 그것이 내가 슬픈 이유이다. (why, I am, sad)

➜ ______________________.

13. 눈이 내리게 해 주세요! (let, snow)

➜ ______________________!

14. 유감이지만 그것은 고장 났어. (broken)

➜ Sorry, but ______________________.

15. 오늘은 매우 더워. (very hot, today)

➜ ______________________.

16. 그것은 월요일에 고쳐질 거야. (will be fixed)

➜ ______________________ on Monday.

17. 우리는 이번 주말에 축구를 할 것이다. (will play soccer, weekend)

➜ ______________________.

18. 나는 저 생각에 동의한다. (agree with, idea)

➜ ______________________.

19. 어제는 눈이 왔다. (snowed, yesterday)

➜ ______________________.

20. 이건 실제 세상이야! (the real world)

➜ ______________________!

정답과 해설 p.9

Let's Practice More!

SET 01

학습목표 1 | 가리키는 대상에 따라 알맞은 지시대명사를 써요. 공부한 날 : 맞은 개수 : /12개

다음 우리말 뜻과 같도록 ( ) 안에서 알맞은 지시대명사를 고르세요.

01. Who is (this / that) in this photo? 이 사진 속의 이 사람은 누구니?

02. (This / That) is why I am sad. 그게 내가 슬픈 이유야.

03. (This / That) is your grandfather. 저 분은 너의 할아버지이셔.

04. (This / That) is the real world. 이것은 실제 세상이야.

05. (This / That) is your father's diary. 저것은 너희 아버지의 일기장이야.

06. (This / That) made my jaw drop. 저것은 내 입을 떡 벌어지게 했어.

07. (This / That) is called Sirius. 저것은 시리우스라고 불려.

08. (This / That) is my friend. 이 사람은 나의 친구이다.

09. (This / That) is his mother. 이 분은 그의 어머니야.

10. (This / That) is yours. 저것은 너의 것이야.

11. (This / That) is so funny. 이것은 매우 재미있어.

12. (This / That) is really dirty. 저것은 정말 지저분해.

정답과 해설 p.9

Let's Practice More!

SET 02

학습목표 1 | 가리키는 대상에 따라 알맞은 지시대명사를 써요. 공부한 날 : 맞은 개수 : /14개

다음 우리말 뜻과 같도록 빈칸에 This 또는 These 중 알맞은 것을 쓰세요.

01. These are my friends. 이 사람들은 내 친구들이야.

02. ________ is my brother, Sihu. 이 사람은 내 남동생 시후야.

03. ________ are my parents. 이 분들은 나의 부모님이셔.

04. ________ is his diary. 이것은 그의 일기장이야.

05. ________ is my homeroom teacher. 이 분은 나의 담임 선생님이셔.

06. ________ are my pets. 이것들은 나의 애완동물들이야.

07. ________ is her notebook. 이것은 그녀의 공책이야.

08. ________ are his albums. 이것들은 그의 앨범들이야.

09. ________ is so scary. 이것은 매우 무서워.

10. ________ are theirs. 이것들은 그들의 것이야.

11. ________ are my socks. 이것들은 나의 양말이야.

12. ________ is so easy. 이것은 매우 쉬워.

13. ________ are my pants. 이것들은 나의 바지야.

14. ________ is ours. 이것은 우리의 것이야.

정답과 해설 p.9

Let's Practice More!

SET 03

학습목표 1 | 가리키는 대상에 따라 알맞은 지시대명사를 써요. 공부한 날 : 맞은 개수 : /14개

다음 우리말 뜻과 같도록 빈칸에 That 또는 Those 중 알맞은 것을 쓰세요.

01. ___That___ is her idea. 저건 그녀의 생각이야.

02. __________ is called Sirius. 저것은 시리우스라고 불려.

03. __________ are so funny. 저것들은 매우 웃겨.

04. __________ is my grandfather. 저 분은 나의 할아버지이셔.

05. __________ are his photos. 저것들은 그의 사진들이야.

06. __________ is our cat. 저것은 우리의 고양이야.

07. __________ is his old camera. 저것은 그의 오래된 카메라야.

08. __________ are my sisters. 저 사람들은 나의 자매들이야.

09. __________ are yours. 저것들은 너의 것이야.

10. __________ is about history. 저것은 역사에 관한 것이야.

11. __________ are really beautiful. 저것들은 정말 아름다워.

12. __________ is a raincoat. 저것은 비옷이야.

13. __________ are my cousins. 저 사람들은 나의 사촌들이야.

14. __________ are his glasses. 저것들은 그의 안경이야.

정답과 해설 p.9

Let's Practice More!

SET 04

학습목표 2 | 가리키는 대상에 따라 알맞은 지시형용사를 써요. 공부한 날 : 맞은 개수 : /12개

다음 우리말 뜻과 같도록 빈칸에 this[This] 또는 these[These] 중 알맞은 것을 쓰세요.

01. Who is this in <u>this</u> photo?
이 사진 속의 이 사람은 누구니?

02. I hope it snows _____ Christmas.
나는 이번 크리스마스에 눈이 오길 바란다.

03. Look at all __________ stars! 이 모든 별들을 봐!

04. __________ books are mine. 이 책들은 나의 것이야.

05. Christmas is on Friday __________ year. 올해 크리스마스는 금요일이야.

06. Did you make all __________ things? 네가 이 모든 것들을 만들었니?

07. __________ pencil is yours. 이 연필은 너의 것이야.

08. Where did you find __________ bag? 너는 이 가방을 어디에서 찾았니?

09. I like __________ photos. 나는 이 사진들이 좋아.

10. Sorry, but __________ car is broken. 유감이지만 이 차는 고장났어.

11. __________ book was in that bag. 이 책은 저 가방 안에 있었어.

12. We will play soccer __________ weekend. 우리는 이번 주말에 축구를 할 거야.

정답과 해설 p.10

Let's Practice More!

SET 05

학습목표 2 | 가리키는 대상에 따라 알맞은 지시형용사를 써요. 공부한 날 : 맞은 개수 : /14개

다음 우리말 뜻과 같도록 빈칸에 that[That] 또는 those[Those] 중 알맞은 것을 쓰세요.

01. ___That___ man is your grandfather. 저 남자 분은 너의 할아버지이셔.

02. It was in ________ book. 그것은 저 책 속에 있었어.

03. All ________ stars are shining. 저 모든 별들은 빛나고 있어.

04. ________ diary made my jaw drop. 저 일기장은 내 입을 떡 벌어지게 했어.

05. What is the name of ________ star? 저 별의 이름이 뭐니?

06. All ________ stars are beautiful. 저 모든 별들은 아름다워.

07. What is ________ book about? 저 책은 무슨 내용이니?

08. ________ star is called Sirius. 저 별은 시리우스라고 불려.

09. I found it between ________ books. 나는 그것을 저 책들 사이에서 찾았어.

10. ________ choice is strange. 저 선택은 이상해.

11. ________ diary is his. 저 일기장은 그의 것이야.

12. Who is ________ girl? 저 소녀는 누구니?

13. ________ people are firefighters. 저 사람들은 소방관들이야.

14. I agree with ________ idea. 나는 저 생각에 동의해.

정답과 해설 p.10

Let's Practice More!

SET 06

학습목표 3 | 지시대명사와 지시형용사를 구분해 보아요. 공부한 날 : 맞은 개수 : /14개

밑줄 친 부분이 지시대명사면 '대', 지시형용사면 '형'이라고 빈칸에 쓰세요.

01. This planetarium is dark inside. 이 천문관은 내부가 어둡다. → 형

02. This show is wonderful. 이 쇼는 멋져. → ______

03. That is so bright. 저것은 매우 밝아. → ______

04. Those are my friends. 저 사람들은 내 친구들이야. → ______

05. I agree with that idea. 나는 저 생각에 동의해. → ______

06. These are my family members. 이 사람들은 나의 가족들이야. → ______

07. These pens are mine. 이 펜들은 나의 것이야. → ______

08. Those are mine. 저것들은 나의 것이야. → ______

09. Did you make all these things? 네가 이 모든 것들을 만들었니? → ______

10. That is my little brother, Sihu. 저 사람은 나의 남동생 시후야. → ______

11. I like those flowers. 난 저 꽃들이 좋아. → ______

12. Look at all these stars! 이 모든 별들을 봐! → ______

13. Those are her new shoes. 저것들은 그녀의 새 신발이야. → ______

14. That is my uncle. 저 사람은 나의 삼촌이야. → ______

정답과 해설 p.10

Let's Practice More!

SET 07

학습목표 4 | 지시대명사 it과 비인칭주어 it을 구분해 보아요. 공부한 날 : 맞은 개수 : /20개

다음 문장의 밑줄 친 it[It]이 지시대명사이면 '지', 비인칭주어이면 '비'라고 쓰세요.

01. It is 7 o'clock.
7시 정각이야.

→ 비

02. It is Christmas Eve.
크리스마스이브다.

→ ______

03. It was an amazing place. 그것은 놀라운 장소였어. → ______

04. It is dark inside. 안쪽은 어두워. → ______

05. I think it will rain. 비가 올 것 같아. → ______

06. It shows me the night sky. 그것은 내게 밤하늘을 보여줘. → ______

07. I see it for the first time. 난 그것을 처음 봐. → ______

08. It is so wonderful. 그것은 매우 멋있어. → ______

09. It is so bright! 매우 밝다! → ______

10. Where do you find it? 너는 어디에서 그것을 찾니? → ______

정답과 해설 p.10

11. I found it between those books. → ____________
난 저 책들 사이에서 그것을 찾았어.

12. What time is it? 몇 시야? → ____________

13. Now, it is winter.
이제 겨울이야.

→ ____________

14. It is my cat.
그것은 나의 고양이야.

→ ____________

15. It is a bright star. 그것은 밝은 별이야. → ____________

16. It is cold today. 오늘 추워. → ____________

17. It is Saturday today. 오늘은 토요일이야. → ____________

18. It is January first. 1월 1일이야. → ____________

19. It is on the table. 그것은 식탁 위에 있어. → ____________

20. It is cloudy today. 오늘은 날이 흐려. → ____________

정답과 해설 p.10

Let's Practice More!

SET 08

학습목표 5 | 지시대명사와 지시형용사, 비인칭주어 it의 쓰임을 익혀 보아요. 공부한 날 : 맞은 개수 : /20개

다음 우리말 뜻과 같도록 빈칸에 알맞은 단어를 쓰세요.

01. ___This___ made my jaw drop.
이것은 내 입이 떡 벌어지게 했어.

02. ________ looks old.
그것은 오래 되어 보여.

03. ________ is 7 o'clock. 7시 정각이야.

04. ________ are her glasses. 저것들은 그녀의 안경이야.

05. ________ star is shining. 저 별은 빛나고 있어.

06. What is the name of ________ boy? 저 남자애의 이름은 무엇이니?

07. ________ flowers are for my mother. 이 꽃들은 우리 어머니를 위한 거야.

08. Look at ________ animals! 저 동물들을 봐!

09. Did you make ________ cake? 네가 이 케이크를 만들었니?

10. Where did you find ________? 넌 어디서 그것을 찾았니?

정답과 해설 p.10

11. __________ is my friend, Mike. 저 사람은 내 친구인 Mike야.

12. __________ snowed yesterday. 어제 눈이 왔어.

13. We will play soccer __________ weekend. 우리는 이번 주말에 축구를 할 거야.

14. __________ are my friends. 이 사람들은 내 친구들이야.

15. Watch out! __________ are broken.
조심해! 이것들은 깨졌어.

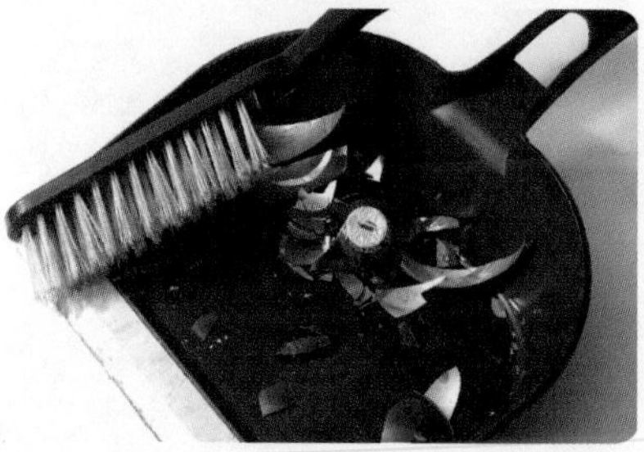

16. I found my hamster between __________ boxes.
난 내 햄스터를 저 상자들 사이에서 찾았어.

17. __________ is my sister's smartphone. 저것은 내 여동생의 스마트폰이야.

18. __________ computers will be fixed on Monday. 이 컴퓨터들은 월요일에 고쳐질 거야.

19. __________ is his computer. 이것은 그의 컴퓨터야.

20. Tell me about __________. 이것들에 대해 나에게 말해봐.

정답과 해설 p.10

Chapter 05 be동사

이 챕터에서는 'be동사'에 대해 익히고,
be동사의 형태 변화에 대해 배워 봐요.

☆ 학습 방향 및 배울 내용 미리보기 ☆

☐ **Unit 01 : I am** a genius.

주어에 따라 다른 be동사

be동사가 주어에 따라 어떻게 달라지는지 알려줄게요.

▼

☐ **Unit 02 : I am** hungry.

be동사의 우리말 뜻

be동사는 어떻게 해석하는지 알아보고, be동사의 줄임말에 대해 배워 봐요.

단어 미리보기

이 챕터에 나올 단어들 중 이미 알고 있는 단어가 있나요?
맞는 뜻을 골라 체크해 봐요.

날짜 : 이름 : 알고 있는 단어의 수 : /24개

No.	아는 단어	단어	품사	알맞은 뜻에 체크 표시해 봐요.			
1	☑	winner	명사	승자	☑	패자	☐
2	☐	twins	명사	쌍둥이	☐	별자리	☐
3	☐	dog	명사	고양이	☐	개	☐
4	☐	jellyfish	명사	젤리	☐	해파리	☐
5	☐	small	형용사	큰	☐	작은	☐
6	☐	kitchen	명사	부엌	☐	닭	☐
7	☐	jail	명사	감옥	☐	항아리	☐
8	☐	park	명사	나무	☐	공원	☐
9	☐	tired	형용사	피곤한	☐	생기 있는	☐
10	☐	class	명사	수업	☐	학교	☐
11	☐	drive	동사	날다	☐	운전하다	☐
12	☐	tall	형용사	키가 작은	☐	키가 큰	☐
13	☐	clever	형용사	서투른	☐	똑똑한	☐
14	☐	mean	형용사	정직한	☐	못된	☐
15	☐	seat	명사	자리	☐	안전벨트	☐
16	☐	floor	명사	층	☐	벽	☐
17	☐	best	형용사	최고의	☐	최악의	☐
18	☐	alone	부사	혼자	☐	함께	☐
19	☐	fat	형용사	날씬한	☐	뚱뚱한	☐
20	☐	hobby	명사	취미	☐	습관	☐
21	☐	favorite	형용사	매우 싫어하는	☐	매우 좋아하는	☐
22	☐	liar	명사	거짓말쟁이	☐	진실	☐
23	☐	pool	명사	수영장	☐	바보	☐
24	☐	stranger	명사	아는 사람	☐	처음 온 사람	☐

주어에 따라 다른 be동사

UNIT 01 I am a genius.

be동사는 am/are/is로 주어에 따라 알맞은 형태가 달라요!

❖ POiNT 1 ❖

1인칭	I	am
2인칭	You	are

I am a genius. 나는 천재야.

You are a star. 너는 스타야.

You are grown-ups. 당신들은 어른이에요.

❖ POiNT 2 ❖

3인칭 단수 (하나)	He / She	is
	It / This / That	

He is a champion. 그가 챔피언이야.

She is a winner. 그녀가 우승자야.

This is a present for you. 이건 널 위한 선물이야.

The case is for an iPhone. 그 케이스는 아이폰용이에요.

❖ POiNT 3 ❖

복수 (여럿)	We	are
	They	

We are twins. 우리는 쌍둥이들이야.

You and I are good friends. 너와 나는 좋은 친구들이야.

They are my parents. 그들은 나의 부모님이셔.

Dogs are our best friends. 개들은 우리의 제일 좋은 친구야.

Check and Write

다음 문장을 보고 [ ] 에 들어갈 말을 쓰세요.

1. That [is] a jellyfish.
   저것은 해파리야.

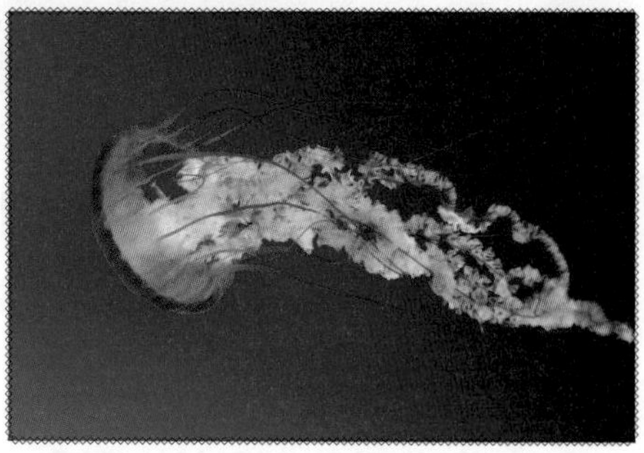

2. They [ ] so funny.
   그들은 매우 웃겨.

3. My brother [ ] a big eater.
   우리 형은 대식가야.

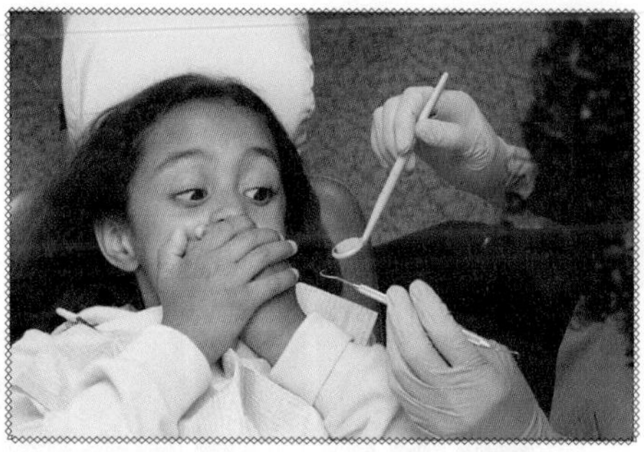

4. I [ ] scared.
   나는 무서워.

5. We [ ] heroes!
   우리는 영웅들이야!

6. That cat [ ] very small!
   저 고양이는 매우 작아!

정답과 해설 p.10

UNIT

be동사의 우리말 뜻

02 I am hungry.

be동사는 '~(이)다'라고 해석할 때도, '~(에) 있다'고 해석할 때도 있어요!

❖ POiNT 1 ❖

'~(이)다' 라고 해석하는 경우

주어와 같은 것을 뜻해요!

Ms. Brown is my homeroom teacher.

A B

Brown 선생님은 나의 담임선생님이셔. (Brown 선생님 = 나의 담임선생님)

주어의 상태를 나타내요!

I am hungry.

나는 배고프다.

❖ POiNT 2 ❖

'~(에) 있다' 라고 해석하는 경우

He is in jail.

그는 감옥에 있어.

My parents are downstairs.

우리 부모님은 아래층에 계셔.

❖ POiNT 3 ❖

be동사 줄여 쓰기 일상생활에서 '주어+be동사'는 보통 줄여서 써요!

I am	You are	She is	He is	It is	We are	They are
I'm	You're	She's	He's	It's	We're	They're

Check and Write

A 다음 문장에서 밑줄 친 be동사의 알맞은 의미를 골라 ○표 하세요.

1. He <u>is</u> my father.
   → (~이다 / ~에 있다)

2. My mom <u>is</u> in the kitchen.
   → (~이다 / ~에 있다)

3. My little brother <u>is</u> very small!
   → (~이다 / ~에 있다)

4. My dog <u>is</u> in the basket.
   → (~이다 / ~에 있다)

B 다음 문장의 밑줄 친 부분을 줄여서 전체 문장을 다시 쓰세요.

1. <u>I am</u> a superman. 나는 슈퍼맨이야.
   I'm a superman.

2. <u>She is</u> shy. 그녀는 수줍어해.
   ____

3. <u>They are</u> in the amusement park.
   그들은 놀이공원에 있어.
   ____

정답과 해설 p.10

Practice 1 주어에 알맞은 be동사(am, are, is)를 익혀 보아요.

주어진 우리말 뜻을 참고하여 알맞은 형태의 be동사(am, are, is)를 빈칸에 쓰세요.

A At home

1. I ____am____ so tired. 나 너무 피곤해요.

2. Nayeon went early. 나연이는 일찍 갔어.
   She __________ not lazy. 그녀는 게으르지 않아.

3. My phone __________ dead. 제 전화기가 꺼져 있어요.
   I didn't hear the alarm. 전 알람을 못 들었어요.

4. I __________ late for class! 나 수업에 늦었어요!

5. You __________ late again! 너 또 지각이구나!
   I'll drive you to school. 내가 학교에 태워다 줄게.

6. Mom, you __________ my guardian angel!
   엄만 내 수호천사야!

7. You __________ my last hope!
   당신이 내 마지막 희망이에요!

B Twins

1. Incheon __________ our hometown. 인천은 우리 고향이야.

2. Nari __________ nine years old. 나리는 9살이야.

정답과 해설 p.10

3. I ___________ nine years old, too. 나도 9살이야.

4. We ___________ twins. 우리는 쌍둥이야.

5. She ___________ tall. 그녀는 키가 커.

6. But, I ___________ not tall. 그러나 나는 키가 크지 않아.

C In the classroom

1. Mina ___________ nice to everyone. 미나는 모두에게 친절해.

2. Sihu ___________ clever. 시후는 똑똑하다.

3. But, he ___________ so mean. 그러나 그는 너무 못됐어.

4. He ___________ my neighbor. 그는 내 짝이야.

5. Our seats ___________ next to each other.
우리 자리는 나란히 붙어 있어.

6. They ___________ my classmates. 그들은 나의 반 친구들이야.

7. We ___________ in the same class.
우리는 같은 반이야.

정답과 해설 p.10

Practice 2 be동사를 사용한 문장을 완성해 보아요.

우리말 해석에 맞도록 괄호 안의 표현을 순서에 맞게 배열하여 문장을 완성하세요.

1. (are, Vegetables, good) for your health. (*be good for: ~에 좋다)
채소는 너의 건강에 좋아.

➔ Vegetables are good for your health.

2. (am, thirsty, I).
나 목말라.

➔ ______________________.

3. (is, curry, Today's dinner). 오늘 저녁은 카레야.
➔ ______________________.

4. (is, The dessert, in the fridge). (*fridge: 냉장고) 디저트는 냉장고에 있어.
➔ ______________________.

5. (am, full, I). 나 배불러요.
➔ ______________________.

6. (on the first floor, is, The cafe). 그 카페는 1층에 있어.
➔ ______________________.

7. (is, My computer, old). 내 컴퓨터는 낡았어.
➔ ______________________.

8. (brand new, is, This mobile phone). 이 휴대폰은 신상품이야.
➔ ______________________.

9. (cartoon characters, Superman and Batman, are).
슈퍼맨과 배트맨은 만화 캐릭터야.
➔ ______________________.

정답과 해설 p.10

10. ("Zootopia," the best movie ever, is). '주토피아'는 역대 최고의 영화야.

➔ ______________________________.

11. No, (is, "Shrek," the best movie). 아니야, '슈렉'이 최고의 영화야.

➔ No, ______________________________.

12. (is, my hero, Iron Man). 아이언맨은 내 영웅이야.

➔ ______________________________.

13. (better off alone, am, I). 나는 혼자 있는 게 나아.

➔ ______________________________.

14. (are, mad or scared, They). 그들은 화나 있거나 두려워하고 있다.

➔ ______________________________.

15. (so stressed, is, Your dad). 너의 아빠는 몹시 스트레스를 받으셨어.

➔ ______________________________.

16. (You, best friend, my, are). 네가 나의 최고의 친구야.

➔ ______________________________.

17. (are, These penguins, so cute). 이 펭귄들은 정말 귀엽다.

➔ ______________________________

______________________________.

18. (a slow walker, I, am), but I never walk back. 나는 느리게 걷는 사람이지만 절대 후퇴하지 않는다.

* Abraham Lincoln(에이브러햄 링컨)

➔ ______________________________,

but I never walk back.

CH 05

Practice 3 알맞은 be동사를 써서 완전한 문장을 써 보아요.

우리말 뜻을 참고하여 주어진 표현을 사용해 문장을 완성해 보세요.

1. (dead) 그의 전화기는 꺼져 있어.

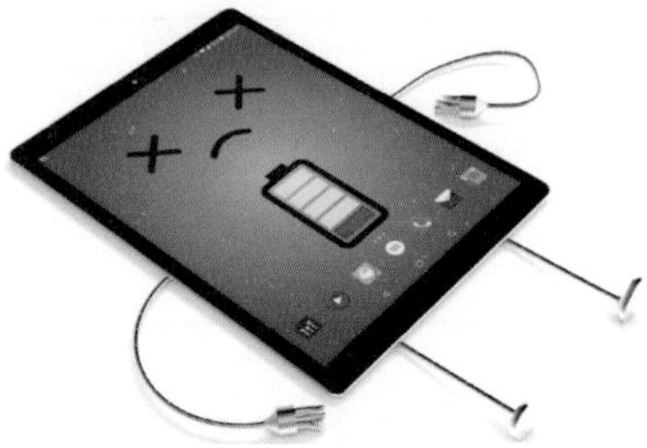

➔ His phone is dead.

2. (in a meeting) 아빠는 회의 중이야.

➔ ____________________.

3. (at home, now) 나 지금 집에 있어.

➔ ____________________.

4. (two hours late) 난 2시간 늦었어.

➔ ____________________.

5. (a visitor) 난 방문자야.

➔ ____________________.

6. (a stranger, here) 나는 여기가 처음이야.

➔ ____________________.

7. (the line, busy) (*busy: 통화 중인) 통화 중입니다.

➔ ____________________.

8. (teacher) 그녀는 선생님이야.

➔ ____________________.

9. (short) 그는 키가 작아.

➔ ____________________.

정답과 해설 p.10

10. (in the kitchen) 내 어머니는 부엌에 계셔.

➔ ____.

11. (The kids, in the pool) 아이들은 수영장에 있어.

➔ ____.

12. (The final test, around the corner) 기말시험이 다가왔어.

➔ ____.

13. (The holiday, on Friday) 휴일은 금요일이야.

➔ ____.

14. (clever) 넌 똑똑해.

➔ ____.

15. (a liar) 넌 거짓말쟁이야!

➔ ______________________________!

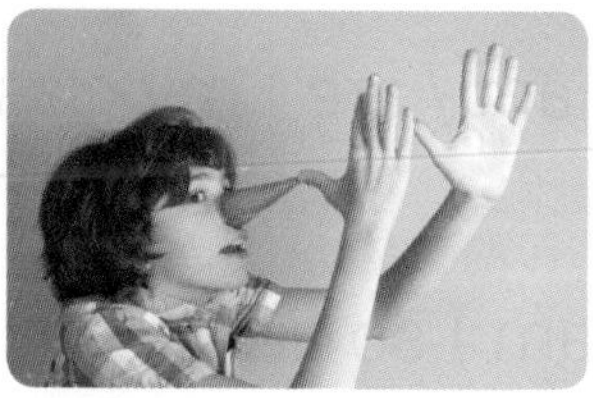

16. (Korean) 우리는 한국인이다.

➔ ____.

17. (My hobby, reading webcomics) 내 취미는 웹툰 보는 거야.

➔ ____.

18. (the best basketball player) 그는 최고의 농구 선수야.

➔ ____.

19. (my favorite singer) 그녀는 내가 가장 좋아하는 가수야.

➔ ____.

CH 05

정답과 해설 p.11

Let's Practice More!

SET 01

학습목표 1 | 주어에 따라 달라지는 be동사를 익혀 보아요. 공부한 날 : 맞은 개수 : /12개

다음 ( ) 안에서 알맞은 be동사(am, are, is)를 고르세요.

01. We (is / are) twins.
우리는 쌍둥이야.

02. We (am / are) in the same class.
우리는 같은 반이야.

03. I (am / are) full. 나 배불러요.

04. She (are / is) tall. 그녀는 키가 커.

05. They (am / are) my classmates. 그들은 나의 반 친구들이야.

06. I (is / am) so tired. 나 너무 피곤해요.

07. You (am / are) my last hope! 당신이 내 마지막 희망이에요!

08. He (is / are) short. 그는 키가 작아.

09. I (are / am) not tall. 나는 키가 크지 않아.

10. She (am / is) kind. 그녀는 친절해.

11. He (are / is) so mean. 그는 너무 못됐어.

12. They (are / is) so funny. 그들은 매우 웃겨.

정답과 해설 p.11

Let's Practice More!

SET 02

학습목표 1 | **주어에 따라 달라지는 be동사를 익혀 보아요.** 공부한 날 : 맞은 개수 : /14개

다음 ( ) 안에서 알맞은 be동사(am, are, is)를 고르세요.

01. Your dad (are / is) in a meeting. 너의 아빠는 회의 중이셔.

02. Vegetables (is / are) good for your health. 야채는 건강에 좋아.

03. Superman and Batman (am / are) cartoon characters. 슈퍼맨과 배트맨은 만화 캐릭터야.

04. The cafe (are / is) on the first floor. 그 카페는 1층에 있어요.

05. The kids (are / is) in the pool. 아이들은 수영장에 있어.

06. The final test (am / is) around the corner. 기말시험이 다가왔어.

07. That cat (am / is) very small. 저 고양이는 매우 작아.

08. Our seats (are / is) next to each other. 우리 자리는 나란히 붙어 있어.

09. Iron Man (am / is) my hero. 아이언맨은 나의 영웅이야.

10. These penguins (are / is) so cute. 이 펭귄들 정말 귀엽다.

11. Incheon (am / is) our hometown. 인천은 우리 고향이야.

12. Mina (is / are) nice to everyone. 미나는 모두에게 친절해.

13. We (am / are) Korean. 우리는 한국 사람이야.

14. Today's dinner (is / are) curry. 오늘 저녁은 카레야.

정답과 해설 p.11

Let's Practice More!

SET 03

학습목표 1 | 주어에 따라 달라지는 be동사를 익혀 보아요. 공부한 날 : 맞은 개수 : /14개

문장의 빈칸에 알맞은 be동사(am, are, is)를 쓰세요.

01. I ___am___ so tired.
나 너무 피곤해요.

02. The dessert ________ in the fridge.
디저트는 냉장고에 있어.

03. I ________ late for school. 나 학교에 늦었어요.

04. You ________ my guardian angel. 너는 내 수호천사야.

05. Ms. Kim ________ my homeroom teacher. 김선생님은 나의 담임선생님이셔.

06. His phone ________ dead. 그의 전화기는 꺼져있어.

07. They ________ in the same class. 그들은 같은 반이야.

08. The line ________ busy. 통화 중입니다.

09. We ________ friends. 우리는 친구야.

10. The holiday ________ on Friday. 휴일은 금요일이야.

11. They ________ mad. 그들은 화가 나 있다.

12. Mina ________ scared. 미나는 두려워한다.

13. I ________ a visitor. 난 방문자야.

14. You ________ a stranger here. 너는 여기가 처음이야.

정답과 해설 p.11

Let's Practice More!

SET 04

학습목표 1 | 주어에 따라 달라지는 be동사를 익혀 보아요. 공부한 날 : 맞은 개수 : /12개

다음 ( ) 안에서 알맞은 주격인칭대명사(I, You, He, She, We, They)를 고르세요.

01. (I / you) am thirsty.
나 목말라.

02. (You / She) are a liar!
넌 거짓말쟁이야!

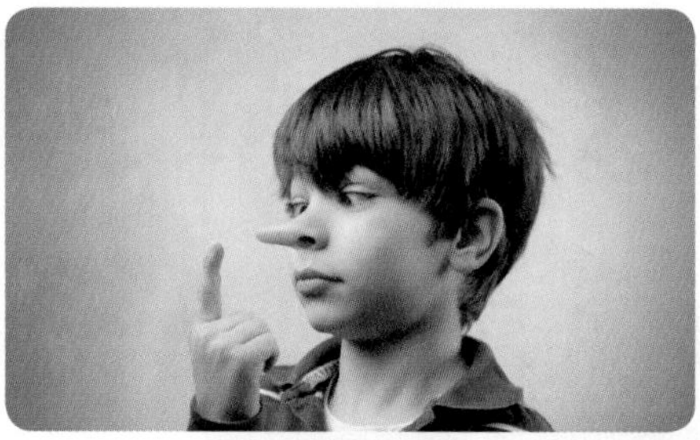

03. (I / She) is clever. 그녀는 똑똑하다.

04. (You / I) am nine years old. 나는 9살이야.

05. (He / They) is nice to everyone. 그는 모두에게 친절해.

06. (We / She) are late. 우리는 늦었어.

07. (They / I) are two hours late. 그들은 두 시간 늦었어.

08. (He / You) is my neighbor. 그는 내 짝이야.

09. (We / I) am a slow walker. 난 느리게 걷는 사람이다.

10. (He / You) are fast. 너는 빨라.

11. (They / I) are at home now. 그들은 지금 집에 있어.

12. (We / He) is my best friend. 그는 나의 가장 친한 친구이다.

정답과 해설 p.11

Let's Practice More!

SET 05

학습목표 1 | 주어에 따라 달라지는 be동사를 익혀 보아요. 공부한 날 : 맞은 개수 : /14개

다음 우리말 뜻을 참고하여 문장의 빈칸에 알맞은 주어와 be동사(am, are, is)를 쓰세요.

01. ___I___ ___am___ hungry.
나는 배가 고파.

02. ________ ________ my neighbor.
그녀는 내 짝이야.

03. ________ ________ lazy. 그는 게으르다.

04. ________ ________ my classmates. 그들은 나의 반 친구들이야.

05. ________ ________ so kind. 그녀는 매우 친절해.

06. ________ ________ better off alone. 난 혼자 있는 게 나아.

07. ________ ________ my lovely son. 넌 나의 사랑스런 아들이다.

08. ________ ________ old. 그것은 오래됐어.

09. ________ ________ so funny. 그는 매우 웃겨.

10. ________ ________ late again. 우리 또 지각이야.

11. ________ ________ busy. 그들은 바빠.

12. ________ ________ thirsty. 나는 목말라.

13. ________ ________ the best movie ever. 그것은 역대 최고의 영화야.

14. ________ ________ my favorite actor. 그는 내가 가장 좋아하는 배우야.

정답과 해설 p.11

Let's Practice More!

SET 06

학습목표 2 | be동사를 주어와 함께 줄여서 쓸 수 있어요. 공부한 날 : 맞은 개수 : /14개

다음 문장의 밑줄 친 부분을 줄여서 다시 쓰세요.

01. <u>I am</u> so tired. 나 너무 피곤해요. → I'm so tired.

02. <u>He is</u> in a meeting. 그는 회의 중이야. → ________ in a meeting.

03. <u>She is</u> short. 그녀는 키가 작아. → ________ short.

04. <u>We are</u> hungry. 우리는 배가 고파. → ________ hungry.

05. <u>They are</u> scared. 그들은 두려워한다. → ________ scared.

06. <u>She is</u> my favorite singer. 그녀는 내가 가장 좋아하는 가수야. → ________ my favorite singer.

07. <u>You are</u> so thin. 너는 정말 날씬해. → ________ so thin.

08. <u>I am</u> at home. 나는 집에 있어. → ________ at home.

09. <u>They are</u> cartoon characters. 그것들은 만화 캐릭터야. → ________ cartoon characters.

10. <u>He is</u> so cute. 그는 정말 귀엽다. → ________ so cute.

11. <u>They are</u> Japanese. 그들은 일본 사람이다. → ________ Japanese.

12. <u>We are</u> friends. 우리는 친구야. → ________ friends.

13. <u>I am</u> nine years old. 나는 9살이야. → ________ nine years old.

14. <u>It is</u> very small. 그것은 매우 작아. → ________ very small.

정답과 해설 p.11

Let's Practice More!

SET 07

학습목표 3 | be동사의 우리말 뜻을 익혀 보아요. 공부한 날 : 맞은 개수 : /20개

다음 문장의 밑줄 친 be동사(am, are, is)의 의미로 알맞은 것을 고르세요.

01. My mother is in the kitchen. (~이다 / ~에 있다)

02. The kids are on the playground. (~이다 / ~에 있다)

03. They are busy. (~이다 / ~에 있다)

04. Mr. Lee is my homeroom teacher. (~이다 / ~에 있다)

05. We are twins. (~이다 / ~에 있다)

06. I am tall. (~이다 / ~에 있다)

07. My dad is downstairs. (~이다 / ~에 있다)

08. You are my best treasure. (~이다 / ~에 있다)

09. He is in jail. (~이다 / ~에 있다)

10. She is clever. (~이다 / ~에 있다)

11. The dog is on the sofa. (~이다 / ~에 있다)

12. We are in the living room. (~이다 / ~에 있다)

13. I am a slow walker. (~이다 / ~에 있다)

14. The cake is in the fridge. (~이다 / ~에 있다)

15. Those cats are mine. (~이다 / ~에 있다)

16. Today's lunch is Bulgogi. (~이다 / ~에 있다)

17. Your notebooks are on the desk. (~이다 / ~에 있다)

18. This doll is yours. (~이다 / ~에 있다)

19. He is so funny. (~이다 / ~에 있다)

20. They are in the pool. (~이다 / ~에 있다)

정답과 해설 p.11

Let's Practice More!

SET 08

학습목표 4 | be동사를 사용해 문장을 완성해 보아요. 공부한 날 : 맞은 개수 : /20개

다음 우리말 해석에 맞도록 빈칸을 채워 문장을 완성해 보세요.

01. She is my favorite singer.
그녀는 내가 가장 좋아하는 가수야.

02. ________ ________ the ________ basketball player.
그는 최고의 농구선수야.

03. ________ ________ my ________. 그분들은 나의 부모님이셔.

04. The ________ ________ in the fridge. 디저트는 냉장고에 있어.

05. ________ ________ my little brother, Sihu. 그는 내 남동생 시후야.

06. ________ ________ twins. 우리는 쌍둥이야.

07. The ________ ________ on the ________ floor. 그 카페는 일층에 있어.

08. ________ ________ 2 hours ________. 난 두 시간 늦었다.

09. ________ ________ my guardian angel! 넌 나의 수호천사야!

10. ________ ________ a teacher. 그녀는 선생님이야.

11. ________ penguins ________ so ________. 이 펭귄들 정말 귀엽다.

12. ________ ________ ________ mine. 저 고양이는 내거야.

13. ________ ________ ________ in a meeting. 나의 아빠는 회의 중이셔.

14. The ________ ________ very small. 그 고양이는 매우 작아.

15. ________ ________ good for your health.
채소는 너의 건강에 좋아.

16. ________ ________ full. 나 배불러요.

17. ________ ________ so mean. 그는 너무 못됐어.

18. ________ ________ scared. 그들은 두려워해.

19. ________ ________ at home. 그녀는 집에 있어.

20. The ________ ________ in the pool. 아이들은 수영장에 있어.

정답과 해설 p.11

실전테스트

CHAPTER 03~05

공부한 날 :
복습한 날 :
부모님 확인 :

CHAPTER 03 인칭대명사 CHAPTER 04 지시대명사와 비인칭주어 it CHAPTER 05 be 동사

● 정답과 해설은 별책 11쪽에서 확인하세요!!

[01~04] 다음 그림을 보고, 괄호 안의 단어 중 맞는 것에 ○표 하세요.

01

(They / This) are in my room.

02

It's (she / her) notebook.

03

John takes a picture of (us / we).

04

She calls (his / him).

[05~07] 괄호 안의 단어를 문장에 알맞은 형태의 인칭대명사로 바꾼 것을 고르세요.

05

That ball is __________ . (you)

① you ② your
③ yours ④ mine

06

__________ books are interesting. (they)

① Their ② Theirs
③ They ④ There

07

__________ are my best friends. (you)

① You ② Yours
③ You're ④ Your

08

다음 그림을 보고, 빈칸에 공통으로 들어갈 알맞은 단어를 고르세요.

A: Who are ________?
B: ________ are my friends.

① they[They]　② them[Them]
③ their[Their]　④ theirs[Theirs]

09

다음 글의 빈칸에 들어갈 알맞은 말을 고르세요.

Susie likes English.
________ studies English every day.

① Hers　② She
③ It　④ Her

10

그림을 참고하여 우리말과 뜻이 같도록 주어진 글자로 시작하는 단어를 쓰세요.

Sally: Is this yours? (이것이 네 것이니?)
Minho: No, it's not m________.
(아니, 그것은 내 것이 아니야.)

[11~12] 그림을 참고하여 빈칸에 알맞은 말을 쓰세요.

11

________ are my books.
(이것들은 나의 책들이다.)

12

________ are my toys.
(저것들은 나의 장난감들이다.)

[13~14] 그림을 보고, 괄호 안의 단어 중 맞는 것에 ○표 하세요.

13

(These / This) dolls are mine.

14

(Those / That) bike is for you.

[15~17] 다음 단어를 바르게 배열하여 문장을 쓰세요.

15

(hot / It / summer / is).

⇨ ______________________________

16

(morning / It / Sunday / is).

⇨ ______________________________

17

(It / April / is / 13th).

⇨ ______________________________

18

다음 표의 빈칸에 [보기]의 단어를 알맞게 분류해서 쓰세요.

[보기] this, her, us, those

인칭대명사	지시대명사

19

다음 빈칸에 들어갈 알맞은 단어를 고르세요.

A: Is this your pencil?
B: Yes, it's ________.

① me ② mine ③ my ④ I

20

다음 우리말 해석과 같도록 빈칸에 공통으로 들어갈 말을 고르세요.

· ________ is summer in Korea.
(한국은 여름이다.)
· ________ is very hot.
(매우 덥다.)

① It ② This
③ That ④ When

[21~22] 밑줄 친 부분을 알맞은 인칭대명사로 바꿔 문장을 다시 써 보세요.

21

Sam and I go to school together.

⇨ ______________________________

22

Seven cars are on the street.

⇨ ______________________________

[23~25] 다음 빈칸에 들어갈 알맞은 be동사를 쓰세요.

23

A: Where are you?
B: I __________ in my room.

24

These cats __________ cute.

25

This juice __________ cold.

[26~28] 다음 빈칸에 들어갈 알맞은 단어를 고르세요.

26

This __________ my purse.

① is　② are
③ were　④ am

27

You __________ the best soccer player.

① are　② is
③ am　④ be

28

I __________ not happy.

① is　② am
③ were　④ be

실전테스트

[29~30] 다음 문장의 동사를 바르게 고쳐 다시 쓰세요. (단, 주어는 바꾸지 마세요.)

29

My sister are pretty.

30

You is tall.

정답 p. 12

Game

아래 그림에 해당하는 단어를 찾아 동그라미 하세요.

S	T	C	O	O	K	I	E	S
O	Y	B	M	N	H	A	G	K
C	A	P	X	I	R	Q	U	T
K	C	Z	H	O	U	S	E	Z
S	K	G	R	N	K	Q	S	F
V	S	U	P	T	W	I	A	B
J	P	T	O	Z	D	G	E	L
T	A	I	L	B	P	I	Y	S

초등영문법3800제 LEVEL 1

워크북

WORKBOOK

1. **단어 쓰기 연습** mp3 음성 파일을 듣고 들려주는 단어를 세 번씩 써 보아요.
2. **Dictation Test** mp3 음성 파일을 듣고 빈칸을 채워 보세요.
3. **단어테스트** 단어 쓰기 연습을 하며 암기한 단어들을 제대로 외웠는지 확인해 보아요.
4. **워크북 정답** Dictation Test와 단어테스트의 정답

초등영문법3800제 MP3 파일 이용 방법

1. 홈페이지에서 다운로드

① 마더텅 홈페이지(www.toptutor.co.kr) 접속 → 상단 메뉴 중 [초등 · 유아]의 [교재 소개] 선택
→ 교재 목록에서 해당 교재명 찾아 선택 → 학습자료의 [mp3] 선택 후 다운로드

② 마더텅 홈페이지(www.toptutor.co.kr) 접속 → 상단 메뉴 중 [초등 · 유아] 의 [교재자료실] 선택
→ 자료실 상단의 [교재를 선택하세요.] 에서 해당 교재명 선택
→ 자료 목록에서 mp3 게시물 선택 후 다운로드

2. 모바일 스트리밍 / 다운로드

① 스마트폰으로 교재 뒷면의 QR코드 스캔 → MP3 스트리밍 or 다운로드

② 주소창에 m.toptutor.co.kr 또는 포털에서 '마더텅' 검색 → [MP3 자료실] 선택
→ 상단 메뉴 중 [초등 · 유아] 선택 → 해당 교재명 찾아 선택 후 MP3 스트리밍 or 다운로드

단어 쓰기 연습 1

초3800_1_w1

들려주는 단어를 잘 듣고, 세 번씩 써 보세요.

MP3 1권 단어 01

01 **teacher** 명 선생님	teacher		
02 **student** 명 학생	student		
03 **boy** 명 소년, 남자아이	boy		
04 **girl** 명 소녀, 여자아이	girl		
05 **friend** 명 친구	friend		
06 **park** 명 공원	park		
07 **school** 명 학교	school		
08 **month** 명 달[월]	month		
09 **year** 명 해[연/년]	year		
10 **room** 명 방	room		
11 **house** 명 집	house		
12 **brother** 명 형, 오빠, 남동생	brother		
13 **store** 명 가게, 상점	store		

들려주는 단어를 잘 듣고, 세 번씩 써 보세요.

MP3 1권 단어 01

14 **book** ㊊ 책	book		
15 **umbrella** ㊊ 우산	umbrella		
16 **flower** ㊊ 꽃	flower		
17 **scissors** ㊊ 가위	scissors		
18 **glasses** ㊊ 안경	glasses		
19 **pants** ㊊ 바지	pants		
20 **dish** ㊊ 그릇, 접시	dish		
21 **church** ㊊ 교회	church		
22 **story** ㊊ 이야기	story		
23 **lady** ㊊ 여자분, 여성	lady		
24 **leaf** ㊊ 나뭇잎	leaf		
25 **foot** ㊊ 발	foot		
26 **sheep** ㊊ 양	sheep		

단어 쓰기 연습 2

초3800_1_w2

들려주는 단어를 잘 듣고, 세 번씩 써 보세요.

MP3 1권 단어 02

27 **wash** ⓢ 씻다	wash		
28 **eraser** 명 지우개	eraser		
29 **computer** 명 컴퓨터	computer		
30 **onion** 명 양파	onion		
31 **sofa** 명 소파	sofa		
32 **classroom** 명 교실	classroom		
33 **wear** 동 (안경을) 쓰다, 입다	wear		
34 **catch** 동 잡다	catch		
35 **river** 명 강	river		
36 **miss** 동 놓치다	miss		
37 **refrigerator** 명 냉장고	refrigerator		
38 **yesterday** 부 어제	yesterday		
39 **eat** 동 먹다	eat		

들려주는 단어를 잘 듣고, 세 번씩 써 보세요.

MP3 1권 단어 02

40 **playground** ⓜ 운동장	playground		
41 **snowball fight** ⓜ 눈싸움	snowball fight		
42 **lend** ⓢ 빌려주다	lend		
43 **weekend** ⓜ 주말	weekend		
44 **errand** ⓜ 심부름	errand		
45 **chocolate** ⓜ 초콜릿	chocolate		
46 **born** ⓗ 타고난	born		
47 **artist** ⓜ 예술가	artist		
48 **see** ⓢ 보다	see		
49 **zoo** ⓜ 동물원	zoo		
50 **butterfly** ⓜ 나비	butterfly		
51 **present** ⓜ 선물	present		
52 **really** ⓑ 정말로	really		

단어 쓰기 연습 3

초3800_1_w3

들려주는 단어를 잘 듣고, 세 번씩 써 보세요.

MP3 1권 단어 03

01 **math** ㊐ 수학	math		
02 **like** ㊍ 좋아하다	like		
03 **love** ㊍ 사랑하다	love		
04 **soccer** ㊐ 축구	soccer		
05 **thirsty** ㊎ 목이 마른	thirsty		
06 **need** ㊍ 필요하다	need		
07 **drink** ㊍ 마시다	drink		
08 **refrigerator** ㊐ 냉장고	refrigerator		
09 **basket** ㊐ 바구니	basket		
10 **room** ㊐ 방	room		
11 **eat** ㊍ 먹다	eat		
12 **dinner** ㊐ 저녁(식사)	dinner		
13 **furniture** ㊐ 가구	furniture		

들려주는 단어를 잘 듣고, 세 번씩 써 보세요.

MP3 1권 단어 03

14 **pants** 명 바지	pants		
15 **chair** 명 의자	chair		
16 **paper** 명 종이	paper		
17 **desk** 명 책상	desk		
18 **sheet** 명 한 장	sheet		
19 **round** 형 둥근	round		
20 **birthday** 명 생일	birthday		
21 **basketball** 명 농구	basketball		
22 **usually** 부 보통	usually		
23 **listen** 동 듣다	listen		
24 **make** 동 만들다	make		
25 **lunch** 명 점심(식사)	lunch		
26 **flour** 명 밀가루	flour		

초3800_1_w4

단어 쓰기 연습 4

들려주는 단어를 잘 듣고, 세 번씩 써 보세요.

MP3 1권 단어 **04**

27	**sugar**	명 설탕	sugar	
28	**look**	동 보다	look	
29	**smoke**	명 연기	smoke	
30	**burn**	동 태우다	burn	
31	**again**	부 다시	again	
32	**oil**	명 기름	oil	
33	**pee**	명 오줌	pee	
34	**government**	명 정부	government	
35	**nature**	명 천성	nature	
36	**knowledge**	명 지식	knowledge	
37	**desire**	동 갈망하다, 바라다	desire	
38	**friendship**	명 우정	friendship	
39	**sum**	명 총합	sum	

들려주는 단어를 잘 듣고, 세 번씩 써 보세요.

MP3 1권 단어 04

40 **success** ㊔ 성공	success		
41 **let** ㊐ ~하게 하다	let		
42 **sense** ㊐ 느끼다	sense		
43 **fear** ㊔ 공포심	fear		
44 **sunshine** ㊔ 햇빛	sunshine		
45 **vegetable** ㊔ 야채	vegetable		
46 **plant** ㊔ 식물	plant		
47 **shade** ㊔ 그늘	shade		
48 **dream** ㊔ 꿈	dream		
49 **homework** ㊔ 숙제	homework		
50 **help** ㊔ 도움	help		
51 **situation** ㊔ 상황	situation		
52 **hope** ㊔ 희망	hope		

단어 쓰기 연습 5

초3800_1_w5

들려주는 단어를 잘 듣고, 세 번씩 써 보세요.

MP3 1권 단어 05

01 **shiny** 형 빛나는	shiny		
02 **give** 동 주다	give		
03 **delicious** 형 아주 맛있는	delicious		
04 **together** 부 함께	together		
05 **bright** 형 밝은	bright		
06 **see** 동 보다	see		
07 **picture** 명 사진	picture		
08 **young** 형 어린	young		
09 **worry** 명 걱정	worry		
10 **duty** 명 의무	duty		
11 **cute** 형 귀여운	cute		
12 **shy** 형 수줍어하는	shy		
13 **live** 동 살다	live		

들려주는 단어를 잘 듣고, 세 번씩 써 보세요.

MP3 1권 단어 05

14 **buy** ⑧ 사다	buy		
15 **pretty** ⑱ 예쁜	pretty		
16 **want** ⑧ 원하다	want		
17 **present** ⑲ 선물	present		
18 **cold** ⑱ 추운	cold		
19 **muffler** ⑲ 목도리	muffler		
20 **coat** ⑲ 코트	coat		
21 **lose** ⑧ 잃어버리다	lose		
22 **rise** ⑧ 뜨다	rise		
23 **night** ⑲ 밤	night		
24 **beautiful** ⑱ 아름다운	beautiful		
25 **sky** ⑲ 하늘	sky		
26 **fight** ⑧ 싸우다	fight		

단어 쓰기 연습 6

초3800_1_w6

들려주는 단어를 잘 듣고, 세 번씩 써 보세요.

MP3 1권 단어 06

27 **bathroom** ㉑ 욕실	bathroom		
28 **before** ㉓ ~하기 전에	before		
29 **wear** ㉔ (안경을) 쓰다, 입다	wear		
30 **blind** ㉕ 잘 안 보이는	blind		
31 **bat** ㉑ 박쥐	bat		
32 **glasses** ㉑ 안경	glasses		
33 **cap** ㉑ 모자	cap		
34 **suitcase** ㉑ 여행 가방	suitcase		
35 **kind** ㉕ 친절한	kind		
36 **left** ㉕ 왼쪽의	left		
37 **summer** ㉑ 여름	summer		
38 **awake** ㉕ 깨어 있는	awake		
39 **pet** ㉑ 애완동물	pet		

들려주는 단어를 잘 듣고, 세 번씩 써 보세요.

MP3 1권 단어 **06**

40 **speak** ㉮ 말하다	speak		
41 **advice** ㉮ 조언	advice		
42 **judge** ㉮ 판단하다	judge		
43 **dream** ㉮ 꿈	dream		
44 **heart** ㉮ 마음	heart		
45 **artist** ㉮ 예술가	artist		
46 **neighbor** ㉮ 이웃	neighbor		
47 **priceless** ㉮ 값을 매길 수 없는	priceless		
48 **treasure** ㉮ 보물	treasure		
49 **ground** ㉮ 땅바닥	ground		
50 **late** ㉮ 늦게	late		
51 **crosswalk** ㉮ 횡단보도	crosswalk		
52 **joke** ㉮ 농담	joke		

단어 쓰기 연습 7

초3800_1_w7

들려주는 단어를 잘 듣고, 세 번씩 써 보세요.

MP3 1권 단어 07

01 **awesome** 형 엄청난	awesome		
02 **fever** 명 열	fever		
03 **mess** 명 엉망진창인 상태	mess		
04 **buy** 동 사다	buy		
05 **cook** 동 요리하다	cook		
06 **friend** 명 친구	friend		
07 **classmate** 명 학급 친구	classmate		
08 **lovely** 형 사랑스러운	lovely		
09 **son** 명 아들	son		
10 **remember** 동 기억하다	remember		
11 **forget** 동 잊어버리다	forget		
12 **hate** 동 몹시 싫어하다	hate		
13 **lend** 동 빌려주다	lend		

들려주는 단어를 잘 듣고, 세 번씩 써 보세요.

MP3 1권 단어 07

14 **exercise** 명 운동	exercise		
15 **pajama** 명 잠옷	pajama		
16 **invite** 동 초대하다	invite		
17 **movie** 명 영화	movie		
18 **taste** 동 맛보다	taste		
19 **wait** 동 기다리다	wait		
20 **selfish** 형 이기적인	selfish		
21 **colored** 형 ~한 색깔의	colored		
22 **pencil** 명 연필	pencil		
23 **share** 동 공유하다	share		
24 **ask** 동 부탁하다	ask		
25 **sharpener** 명 ~을 깎는 기구	sharpener		
26 **fan** 명 팬	fan		

초3800_1_w8

단어 쓰기 연습 8

들려주는 단어를 잘 듣고, 세 번씩 써 보세요.

MP3 1권 단어 08

27 **watch** ㉮ 보다	watch		
28 **hope** ㉮ 바라다	hope		
29 **sing** ㉮ 노래하다	sing		
30 **tone-deaf** ㉻ 음치의	tone-deaf		
31 **carry** ㉮ 전하다	carry		
32 **tune** ㉺ 음정	tune		
33 **singer** ㉺ 가수	singer		
34 **envy** ㉮ 부러워하다	envy		
35 **turn** ㉮ (어떤 나이, 시기가) 되다	turn		
36 **give** ㉮ 주다	give		
37 **stuffed** ㉻ 속을 채운	stuffed		
38 **fluffy** ㉻ 보송보송한	fluffy		
39 **name** ㉮ 이름을 지어주다	name		

들려주는 단어를 잘 듣고, 세 번씩 써 보세요.

MP3 1권 단어 08

40 **draw** ⓢ 그리다	draw		
41 **tomorrow** ⓟ 내일	tomorrow		
42 **map** ⓝ 지도	map		
43 **teenager** ⓝ 10대	teenager		
44 **know** ⓢ 알다	know		
45 **think** ⓢ 생각하다	think		
46 **speak** ⓢ 말하다	speak		
47 **fair** ⓐ 공평한	fair		
48 **pursue** ⓢ 좇다, 추구하다	pursue		
49 **courage** ⓝ 용기	courage		
50 **wonderful** ⓐ 아주 멋진	wonderful		
51 **bake** ⓢ 굽다	bake		
52 **call** ⓢ 전화하다	call		

초3800_1_w9

단어 쓰기 연습 9

들려주는 단어를 잘 듣고, 세 번씩 써 보세요.

MP3 1권 단어 09

01 **amazing** 형 놀라운	amazing		
02 **idea** 명 발상	idea		
03 **voice** 명 목소리	voice		
04 **help** 명 도움	help		
05 **socks** 명 양말	socks		
06 **secret** 명 비밀	secret		
07 **tail** 명 꼬리	tail		
08 **soft** 형 부드러운	soft		
09 **ride** 동 타다	ride		
10 **ring** 명 반지	ring		
11 **closet** 명 옷장	closet		
12 **victory** 명 승리	victory		
13 **choice** 명 선택	choice		

들려주는 단어를 잘 듣고, 세 번씩 써 보세요.

MP3 1권 단어 09

14 **pass** ⓢ 전달하다	pass		
15 **dirty** ⓗ 더러운	dirty		
16 **swimsuit** ⓜ 수영복	swimsuit		
17 **excited** ⓗ 신이 난	excited		
18 **notebook** ⓜ 공책	notebook		
19 **wide** ⓗ 넓은	wide		
20 **ruled** ⓗ 줄이 쳐진	ruled		
21 **cap** ⓜ 뚜껑	cap		
22 **character** ⓜ 캐릭터	character		
23 **hair** ⓜ 머리카락	hair		
24 **cut** ⓢ 자르다	cut		
25 **hairdresser** ⓜ 미용사	hairdresser		
26 **first** ⓗ 첫째의	first		

초3800_1_w10

단어 쓰기 연습 10

들려주는 단어를 잘 듣고, 세 번씩 써 보세요.

MP3 1권 단어 10

27 **shorter** ㊝ 더 짧게	shorter		
28 **feel** ㊢ 느끼다	feel		
29 **longer** ㊞ 더 긴	longer		
30 **attention** ㊐ 주의	attention		
31 **aboard** ㊟ ~을 탑승하여	aboard		
32 **fasten** ㊢ 매다	fasten		
33 **seat belt** ㊐ 안전벨트	seat belt		
34 **safety** ㊐ 안전	safety		
35 **question** ㊐ 질문	question		
36 **staff** ㊐ 직원	staff		
37 **eraser** ㊐ 지우개	eraser		
38 **break** ㊢ 부수다	break		
39 **pleasure** ㊐ 기쁨	pleasure		

들려주는 단어를 잘 듣고, 세 번씩 써 보세요.

MP3 1권 단어 10

40 **meet** 동 만나다	meet		
41 **flight** 명 비행	flight		
42 **haircut** 명 이발	haircut		
43 **tray** 명 선반	tray		
44 **full** 형 가득한	full		
45 **position** 명 위치	position		
46 **sleep** 명 잠	sleep		
47 **talk** 동 말하다	talk		
48 **put** 동 놓다	put		
49 **book** 명 책	book		
50 **coach** 명 코치	coach		
51 **ticket** 명 표	ticket		
52 **check** 동 확인하다	check		

초3800_1_w11

단어 쓰기 연습 11

들려주는 단어를 잘 듣고, 세 번씩 써 보세요.

MP3 1권 단어 11

01 **strong** 형 강한	strong		
02 **ugly** 형 못생긴	ugly		
03 **uncle** 명 삼촌	uncle		
04 **afraid** 형 무서운	afraid		
05 **cousin** 명 사촌	cousin		
06 **toy** 명 장난감	toy		
07 **gun** 명 총	gun		
08 **get** 동 얻다, 받다	get		
09 **house** 명 집	house		
10 **doughnut** 명 도넛	doughnut		
11 **candy** 명 사탕	candy		
12 **hungry** 형 배고픈	hungry		
13 **egg** 명 계란	egg		

들려주는 단어를 잘 듣고, 세 번씩 써 보세요.

MP3 1권 단어 11

14 **maybe** 부 아마	maybe		
15 **crocodile** 명 악어	crocodile		
16 **parents** 명 부모	parents		
17 **run** 동 뛰다	run		
18 **late** 형 늦은	late		
19 **snowy** 형 눈이 내리는	snowy		
20 **far** 형 먼	far		
21 **dark** 형 어두운	dark		
22 **light** 명 불	light		
23 **rainy** 형 비가 오는	rainy		
24 **play** 동 놀다	play		
25 **outside** 부 밖에서	outside		
26 **cookie** 명 쿠키	cookie		

초3800_1_w12

단어 쓰기 연습 12

들려주는 단어를 잘 듣고, 세 번씩 써 보세요.

MP3 1권 단어 12

27 **wear** ⓓ 입다	wear		
28 **jacket** ⓜ 재킷	jacket		
29 **winter** ⓜ 겨울	winter		
30 **spring** ⓜ 봄	spring		
31 **hurry** ⓓ 서두르다	hurry		
32 **already** ⓑ 이미	already		
33 **owner** ⓜ 주인	owner		
34 **planetarium** ⓜ 천문관	planetarium		
35 **place** ⓜ 장소	place		
36 **bright** ⓗ 밝은	bright		
37 **inside** ⓑ 안에	inside		
38 **show** ⓓ 보여주다	show		
39 **night** ⓜ 밤	night		

들려주는 단어를 잘 듣고, 세 번씩 써 보세요.

MP3 1권 단어 12

40 **star** ⓜ 별	star		
41 **find** ⓢ 발견하다	find		
42 **milky way** ⓜ 은하수	milky way		
43 **year** ⓜ 해(년)	year		
44 **weekend** ⓜ 주말	weekend		
45 **often** ⓑ 자주	often		
46 **photo** ⓜ 사진	photo		
47 **grandfather** ⓜ 할아버지	grandfather		
48 **cloudy** ⓗ 흐린	cloudy		
49 **put on** 입다	put on		
50 **real** ⓗ 진짜의	real		
51 **common** ⓗ 공통의	common		
52 **choice** ⓜ 선택	choice		

단어 쓰기 연습 13

초3800_1_w13

들려주는 단어를 잘 듣고, 세 번씩 써 보세요.

MP3 1권 단어 **13**

01 **genius** 명 천재	genius		
02 **star** 명 스타	star		
03 **grown-up** 명 어른	grown-up		
04 **champion** 명 우승자	champion		
05 **winner** 명 승자	winner		
06 **case** 명 용기, 통	case		
07 **twins** 명 쌍둥이	twins		
08 **dog** 명 개	dog		
09 **jellyfish** 명 해파리	jellyfish		
10 **funny** 형 웃긴	funny		
11 **scared** 형 무서워 하는	scared		
12 **small** 형 작은	small		
13 **homeroom teacher** 명 담임 선생님	homeroom teacher		

들려주는 단어를 잘 듣고, 세 번씩 써 보세요. MP3 1권 단어 13

14 **jail** 명 감옥	jail		
15 **downstairs** 명 아래층	downstairs		
16 **kitchen** 명 부엌	kitchen		
17 **basket** 명 바구니	basket		
18 **shy** 형 수줍은	shy		
19 **park** 명 공원	park		
20 **tired** 형 피곤한	tired		
21 **early** 부 일찍	early		
22 **lazy** 형 게으른	lazy		
23 **dead** 형 작동하지 않는	dead		
24 **alarm** 명 알람	alarm		
25 **late** 형 늦은	late		
26 **class** 명 수업	class		

단어 쓰기 연습 14

초3800_1_w14

들려주는 단어를 잘 듣고, 세 번씩 써 보세요.

MP3 1권 단어 14

27 **drive** ⓢ 태워다 주다, 운전하다	drive		
28 **school** ⓜ 학교	school		
29 **hometown** ⓜ 고향	hometown		
30 **tall** ⓗ 키가 큰	tall		
31 **clever** ⓗ 똑똑한	clever		
32 **mean** ⓗ 못된	mean		
33 **neighbor** ⓜ 이웃	neighbor		
34 **seat** ⓜ 자리	seat		
35 **thirsty** ⓗ 목마른	thirsty		
36 **dessert** ⓜ 디저트	dessert		
37 **fridge** ⓜ 냉장고	fridge		
38 **cafe** ⓜ 카페	cafe		
39 **brand new** ⓗ 완전 새 것인	brand new		

들려주는 단어를 잘 듣고, 세 번씩 써 보세요.

MP3 1권 단어 14

40 **cartoon** 명 만화	cartoon		
41 **movie** 명 영화	movie		
42 **best** 형 최고의	best		
43 **alone** 부 혼자	alone		
44 **better** 형 더 나은	better		
45 **mad** 형 미친	mad		
46 **stressed** 형 스트레스를 받는	stressed		
47 **penguin** 명 펭귄	penguin		
48 **meeting** 명 회의	meeting		
49 **visitor** 명 방문자	visitor		
50 **stranger** 명 처음 온 사람	stranger		
51 **line** 명 (특정 번호의) 전화	line		
52 **short** 형 키가 작은	short		

초3800_1_d1

Dictation Test 1

MP3 1권 받아쓰기 01

Name : Date : Score : /10

[01~10] 들려주는 문장을 잘 듣고 빈칸에 알맞은 단어를 채워 보세요.

01. They are Sihu's ________________.
그들은 시후의 친구들이다.

02. He caught ________________ ________________ in the river.
그는 강에서 물고기 네 마리를 잡았다.

03. There are ________________ ________________.
꽃 세 송이가 있다.

04. Nayeon missed ________________ ________________ this morning.
나연이는 오늘 아침 버스 두 대를 놓쳤다.

05. Do you see ________________ ________________?
너는 사슴 한 마리를 보니?

06. They are ________________.
그들은 쌍둥이이다.

07. Fish are ________________, not food.
물고기들은 친구들이지, 음식이 아니야.

08. We all make ________________.
우리는 모두 실수를 한다.

09. They are ________________ ________________.
그것들은 여우 두 마리이다.

10. I saw ________________ ________________.
나는 쥐 세 마리를 보았다.

정답 p.228

초3800_1_d2

Dictation Test 2

MP3 1권 받아쓰기 02

Name : Date : Score : /10

[01~10] 들려주는 문장을 잘 듣고 빈칸에 알맞은 단어를 채워 보세요.

01. Close your ________________.

눈을 감아 보세요.

02. ________________ run in the park.

아이들은 공원에서 달린다.

03. Look at the two ________________.

아기 두 명을 봐.

04. It has short ________________.

그것은 짧은 다리들을 가지고 있다.

05. I wear ________________.

나는 안경을 쓴다.

06. I got ________________ ________________.

나는 고양이 한 마리를 얻었다.

07. I don't feel my ________________.

나는 내 발가락이 느껴지지 않는다.

08. My ________________ are wet.

내 양말들은 젖었다.

09. Dad ate ________________ ________________ this morning.

아빠는 오늘 아침 사과 한 개를 드셨다.

10. There is ________________ ________________.

탁자 한 개가 있다.

정답 p.228

초3800_1_d3

Dictation Test 3

MP3 1권 받아쓰기 03

Name : Date : Score : /10

[01~10] 들려주는 문장을 잘 듣고 빈칸에 알맞은 단어를 채워 보세요.

01. Mina is from ________________.

미나는 미국에서 왔다.

02. She likes ________________.

그녀는 영어를 좋아한다.

03. She doesn't like ________________.

그녀는 수학을 좋아하지 않는다.

04. ________________ is great.

사랑은 위대하다.

05. I usually listen to ________________ on Sunday.

나는 보통 일요일에 음악을 듣는다.

06. An ________________ is in the basket.

사과 한 알이 바구니 안에 있다.

07. I drank two ________________ of ________________.

나는 주스 두 잔을 마셨다.

08. My ________________ is round.

내 얼굴은 둥글다.

09. My birthday is in ________________.

내 생일은 3월이다.

10. I like ________________.

나는 토요일을 좋아한다.

정답 p.228

초3800_1_d4

Dictation Test 4

MP3 1권 받아쓰기 04

Name : Date : Score : /10

[01~10] 들려주는 문장을 잘 듣고 빈칸에 알맞은 단어를 채워 보세요.

01. I make ________________ with Mom on Sunday.
나는 일요일에 엄마와 함께 점심을 만든다.

02. We need ________________.
우리는 설탕이 필요하다.

03. It is not ________________.
그것은 물이 아니다.

04. ________________ is not everything.
돈이 모든 것은 아니다.

05. ________________ comes from animals.
고기는 동물들로부터 온다.

06. I have a lot of ________________ to do.
나는 해야 할 많은 숙제가 있다.

07. He likes ________________.
그는 월요일을 좋아한다.

08. A ________________ of ________________ is on the table.
피자 한 조각이 탁자 위에 있다.

09. My mom drinks a ________________ of ________________.
나의 엄마는 커피 한 잔을 드신다.

10. I am ________________ Seoul.
나는 서울에서 왔어.

정답 p.228

초3800_1_d5

Dictation Test 5

MP3 1권 받아쓰기 05

Name : Date : Score : /10

[01~10] 들려주는 문장을 잘 듣고 빈칸에 알맞은 단어를 채워 보세요.

01. I am ______ ______.
나는 학생이다.

02. I need ______ ______.
나는 우산 한 개가 필요하다.

03. Let's buy ______ ______ for Mina!
미나를 위한 케이크 한 개를 사자!

04. Mina gave ______ ______ to me.
미나는 나에게 인형 한 개를 주었다.

05. I saw ______ ______.
나는 사진 한 장을 봤다.

06. I have ______ ______ for you.
나는 너를 위한 선물을 가지고 있다.

07. Every child is ______ ______.
모든 아이들은 예술가이다.

08. She is ______ ______ teacher.
그녀는 영어 선생님이다.

09. I have ______ ______.
나는 개 한 마리를 가지고 있다.

10. I need ______ ______.
나는 자전거 한 대가 필요하다.

정답 p.228

초3800_1_d6

Dictation Test 6

MP3 1권 받아쓰기 06

Name : Date : Score : /10

[01~10] 들려주는 문장을 잘 듣고 빈칸에 알맞은 단어를 채워 보세요.

01. ________ ________ is pretty.
그 인형은 예쁘다.

02. ________ ________ rises at night.
달은 밤에 뜬다.

03. She studies ________.
그녀는 역사를 공부한다.

04. I play ________ ________ every day.
나는 매일 피아노를 친다.

05. We have ________ together every day.
우리는 매일 점심을 같이 먹는다.

06. ________ ________ is sweet.
그 사과는 달콤하다.

07. They play ________ together.
그들은 함께 야구를 한다.

08. I run to ________.
나는 학교로 달려간다.

09. He often plays ________.
그는 보통 축구를 한다.

10. Can you play ________ ________?
너는 바이올린을 연주할 수 있니?

정답 p.228

초3800_1_d7

Dictation Test 7

MP3 1권 받아쓰기 07

Name : Date : Score : /10

[01~10] 들려주는 문장을 잘 듣고 빈칸에 알맞은 단어를 채워 보세요.

01. __________ __________ my dog every day.
나는 매일 내 개를 산책시킨다.

02. __________ __________ our bikes after school.
우리는 방과 후에 자전거를 탄다.

03. __________ watches TV after dinner.
그녀는 저녁식사 후에 TV를 본다.

04. __________ are my lovely sons.
너희들은 내 사랑스러운 아들들이다.

05. __________ gives __________ a stuffed cat.
그는 나에게 고양이 인형을 준다.

06. Exercising is good for __________.
운동을 하는 것은 우리에게 좋다.

07. __________ will give a flower to __________.
나는 그녀에게 꽃 한 송이를 줄 것이다.

08. __________ __________ to taste the cake.
나는 그 케이크를 맛보고 싶다.

09. I have to share __________ with __________.
나는 그것들을 그와 함께 나눠 써야 한다.

10. __________ does not lend it to __________.
그는 나에게 그것을 빌려주지 않는다.

정답 p.228

초3800_1_d8

Dictation Test 8

MP3 1권 받아쓰기 08

Name : Date : Score : /10

[01~10] 들려주는 문장을 잘 듣고 빈칸에 알맞은 단어를 채워 보세요.

01. ________________ is selfish!
그는 이기적이야!

02. ________________ is a big fan of ________________.
그녀는 그것의 열렬한 팬이다.

03. ________________ likes ________________.
그녀는 그것들을 좋아한다.

04. After dinner, ________________ had a chocolate cake.
저녁식사 후에 우리는 초콜릿 케이크를 먹었다.

05. ________________ want to eat ________________.
나는 그것을 먹고 싶다.

06. ________________ must do it yourself.
너는 스스로 그것을 해야 한다.

07. Get used to ________________.
그것에 익숙해져라.

08. My mom bakes cookies for ________________.
나의 엄마는 나를 위해 쿠키들을 구우신다.

09. Mina gave ________________ a gift.
미나는 그에게 선물을 주었다.

10. Mr. Kim teaches ________________.
김 선생님은 우리를 가르치신다.

정답 p.228

초3800_1_d9

Dictation Test 9

MP3 1권 받아쓰기 09

Name : Date : Score : /10

[01~10] 들려주는 문장을 잘 듣고 빈칸에 알맞은 단어를 채워 보세요.

01. Ask one of ______________ staff.
우리 직원들 중 한명에게 물어보세요.

02. Are those ______________ ______________?
저 사람들이 너의 친구들이니?

03. Where is ______________?
너의 것은 어디에 있니?

04. The hairdresser cut ______________ ______________ too short.
그 미용사는 그의 머리를 너무 짧게 잘랐다.

05. She liked ______________ ______________.
그녀는 그녀의 자를 좋아했다.

06. Take off ______________ ______________.
너의 신발을 벗어.

07. That is not ______________.
저것은 나의 것이 아니다.

08. She took ______________ ______________.
그녀는 그의 가방을 가져갔다.

09. I love ______________ songs.
나는 그들의 노래를 좋아한다.

10. ______________ tail is soft.
그것의 꼬리는 부드럽다.

정답 p.228

초3800_1_d10

Dictation Test 10

MP3 1권 받아쓰기 10

Name : Date : Score : /10

[01~10] 들려주는 문장을 잘 듣고 빈칸에 알맞은 단어를 채워 보세요.

01. The coat is ________________.

그 코트는 그녀의 것이다.

02. Did you see ________________ ________________?

너 나의 지우개 봤니?

03. Can I use ________________ ________________?

내가 너의 전화기를 써도 될까?

04. He reads a book in ________________ ________________.

그는 그의 방에서 책을 읽는다.

05. We like ________________ teacher.

우리는 우리의 선생님을 좋아한다.

06. Are those ________________ on the desk?

책상 위에 있는 그것들은 그들의 것이니?

07. The ring is ________________.

그 반지는 그의 것이야.

08. Is this swimsuit ________________?

이 수영복은 그녀의 것이니?

09. ________________ ________________ teaches math.

그들의 선생님은 수학을 가르치신다.

10. The victory is ________________.

승리는 우리의 것이야.

정답 p.228

초3800_1_d11

Dictation Test 11

MP3 1권 받아쓰기 11

Name : Date : Score : /10

[01~10] 들려주는 문장을 잘 듣고 빈칸에 알맞은 단어를 채워 보세요.

01. ________________ is my ________________.
저 사람은 나의 삼촌이다.

02. ________________ is Mina.
이 사람은 미나이다.

03. ________________ is ________________.
추워.

04. ________________ is 9 o'clock.
9시야.

05. ________________ are his glasses.
저것들은 그의 안경이다.

06. ________________ ________________ are mine.
이 책들은 나의 것이다.

07. I like ________________ ________________.
나는 이 사진들이 좋다.

08. What ________________ is ________________ today?
오늘은 무슨 요일이니?

09. ________________ show is wonderful.
이 쇼는 멋있다.

10. It was in ________________ ________________.
그것은 저 책에 있었어.

정답 p.228

초3800_1_d12

Dictation Test 12

MP3 1권 받아쓰기 **12**

Name : Date : Score : /10

[01~10] 들려주는 문장을 잘 듣고 빈칸에 알맞은 단어를 채워 보세요.

01. Look at ________ ________!
저 동물들을 봐!

02. ________ snowed yesterday.
어제 눈이 왔다.

03. ________ diary is his.
저 일기장은 그의 것이다.

04. ________ people are fire fighters.
이 사람들은 소방관들이다.

05. I like ________ ________.
나는 저 꽃들이 좋다.

06. ________ is Saturday today.
오늘은 토요일이다.

07. ________ is my ________.
이 분은 나의 아빠이다.

08. ________ is ________.
어두워.

09. ________ is my raincoat.
저것은 나의 비옷이다.

10. What ________ is ________?
몇 시야?

정답 p.228

초3800_1_d13

Dictation Test 13

MP3 1권 받아쓰기 13

Name : Date : Score : /10

[01~10] 들려주는 문장을 잘 듣고 빈칸에 알맞은 단어를 채워 보세요.

01. My ________ ________ in a meeting.
나의 아빠는 회의 중이시다.

02. ________ ________ a teacher.
그녀는 선생님이다.

03. ________ ________ a stranger here.
나는 여기가 처음이다.

04. My ________ ________ reading webcomics.
내 취미는 웹툰을 읽는 것이다.

05. My ________ ________ in the kitchen.
나의 엄마는 부엌에 계신다.

06. The ________ ________ in the pool.
그 아이들은 수영장에 있다.

07. ________ ________ my last hope!
너는 내 마지막 희망이다!

08. ________ ________ nine years old.
나는 9살이다.

09. ________ ________ twins.
우리는 쌍둥이이다.

10. ________ ________ my neighbor.
그는 내 이웃이다.

정답 p.228

초3800_1_d14

Dictation Test 14

MP3 1권 받아쓰기 **14**

Name : Date : Score : /10

[01~10] 들려주는 문장을 잘 듣고 빈칸에 알맞은 단어를 채워 보세요.

01. ________________ ________________ my classmates.
그들은 내 같은 반 친구들이다.

02. Today's dinner ________________ curry.
오늘 저녁은 카레이다.

03. ________________ ________________ full.
나는 배부르다.

04. The cafe ________________ on the first floor.
그 카페는 일층에 있다.

05. Batman ________________ a cartoon character.
배트맨은 만화 캐릭터이다.

06. ________________ ________________ angry.
그들은 화가 났다.

07. ________________ ________________ my best friend.
너는 나의 가장 친한 친구이다.

08. ________________ ________________ at home now.
우리는 지금 집에 있다.

09. The holiday ________________ on Friday.
휴일은 금요일이다.

10. ________________ ________________ the best basketball player.
그는 가장 훌륭한 농구선수이다.

정답 p.228

단어테스트 1

다음 한글 뜻을 보고 영어 표현을 적으세요. Name : Date : Score : /26

01		명 선생님	14		명 책
02		명 학생	15		명 우산
03		명 소년, 남자아이	16		명 꽃
04		명 소녀, 여자아이	17		명 가위
05		명 친구	18		명 안경
06		명 공원	19		명 바지
07		명 학교	20		명 그릇, 접시
08		명 달[월]	21		명 교회
09		명 해[연/년]	22		명 이야기
10		명 방	23		명 여자분, 여성
11		명 집	24		명 나뭇잎
12		명 형, 오빠, 남동생	25		명 발
13		명 가게, 상점	26		명 양

정답 p.228

단어테스트 2

다음 한글 뜻을 보고 영어 표현을 적으세요. Name : Date : Score : /26

01		동 씻다	14		명 운동장
02		명 지우개	15		명 눈싸움
03		명 컴퓨터	16		동 빌려주다
04		명 양파	17		명 주말
05		명 소파	18		명 심부름
06		명 교실	19		명 초콜릿
07		동 (안경을) 쓰다, 입다	20		형 타고난
08		동 잡다	21		명 예술가
09		명 강	22		동 보다
10		동 놓치다	23		명 동물원
11		명 냉장고	24		명 나비
12		부 어제	25		명 선물
13		동 먹다	26		부 정말로

정답 p.228

단어테스트 3

다음 한글 뜻을 보고 영어 표현을 적으세요. Name : Date : Score : /26

01			명 수학
02			동 좋아하다
03			동 사랑하다
04			명 축구
05			형 목이 마른
06			동 필요하다
07			동 마시다
08			명 냉장고
09			명 바구니
10			명 방
11			동 먹다
12			명 저녁(식사)
13			명 가구
14			명 바지
15			명 의자
16			명 종이
17			명 책상
18			명 한 장
19			형 둥근
20			명 생일
21			명 농구
22			부 보통
23			동 듣다
24			동 만들다
25			명 점심(식사)
26			명 밀가루

정답 p.228

단어테스트 4

다음 한글 뜻을 보고 영어 표현을 적으세요. Name : Date : Score : /26

01 ____ 명 설탕
02 ____ 동 보다
03 ____ 명 연기
04 ____ 동 태우다
05 ____ 부 다시
06 ____ 명 기름
07 ____ 명 오줌
08 ____ 명 정부
09 ____ 명 천성
10 ____ 명 지식
11 ____ 동 갈망하다, 바라다
12 ____ 명 우정
13 ____ 명 총합
14 ____ 명 성공
15 ____ 동 ~하게 하다
16 ____ 동 느끼다
17 ____ 명 공포심
18 ____ 명 햇빛
19 ____ 명 야채
20 ____ 명 식물
21 ____ 명 그늘
22 ____ 명 꿈
23 ____ 명 숙제
24 ____ 명 도움
25 ____ 명 상황
26 ____ 명 희망

정답 p.228

단어테스트 5

다음 한글 뜻을 보고 영어 표현을 적으세요. Name : Date : Score : /26

01	형 빛나는	14	동 사다
02	동 주다	15	형 예쁜
03	형 아주 맛있는	16	동 원하다
04	부 함께	17	명 선물
05	형 밝은	18	형 추운
06	동 보다	19	명 목도리
07	명 사진	20	명 코트
08	형 어린	21	동 잃어버리다
09	명 걱정	22	동 뜨다
10	명 의무	23	명 밤
11	형 귀여운	24	형 아름다운
12	형 수줍어하는	25	명 하늘
13	동 살다	26	동 싸우다

정답 p.229

단어테스트 6

다음 한글 뜻을 보고 영어 표현을 적으세요. Name : Date : Score : /26

01 명 욕실
02 접 ~하기 전에
03 동 (안경을) 쓰다, 입다
04 형 잘 안 보이는
05 명 박쥐
06 명 안경
07 명 모자
08 명 여행 가방
09 형 친절한
10 형 왼쪽의
11 명 여름
12 형 깨어 있는
13 명 애완동물
14 동 말하다
15 명 조언
16 동 판단하다
17 명 꿈
18 명 마음
19 명 예술가
20 명 이웃
21 형 값을 매길 수 없는
22 명 보물
23 명 땅바닥
24 부 늦게
25 명 횡단보도
26 명 농담

정답 p.229

단어테스트 7

다음 한글 뜻을 보고 영어 표현을 적으세요. Name : Date : Score : /26

01		형 엄청난	14		명 운동
02		명 열	15		명 잠옷
03		명 엉망진창인 상태	16		동 초대하다
04		동 사다	17		명 영화
05		동 요리하다	18		동 맛보다
06		명 친구	19		동 기다리다
07		명 학급 친구	20		형 이기적인
08		형 사랑스러운	21		형 ~한 색깔의
09		명 아들	22		명 연필
10		동 기억하다	23		동 공유하다
11		동 잊어버리다	24		동 부탁하다
12		동 몹시 싫어하다	25		명 ~을 깎는 기구
13		동 빌려주다	26		명 팬

정답 p.229

단어테스트 8

다음 한글 뜻을 보고 영어 표현을 적으세요. Name : Date : Score : /26

01		동 보다	14		동 그리다
02		동 바라다	15		부 내일
03		동 노래하다	16		명 지도
04		형 음치의	17		명 10대
05		동 전하다	18		동 알다
06		명 음정	19		동 생각하다
07		명 가수	20		동 말하다
08		동 부러워하다	21		형 공평한
09		동 (어떤 나이, 시기가) 되다	22		동 좇다, 추구하다
10		동 주다	23		명 용기
11		형 속을 채운	24		형 아주 멋진
12		형 보송보송한	25		동 굽다
13		동 이름을 지어주다	26		동 전화하다

정답 p.229

단어테스트 9

다음 한글 뜻을 보고 영어 표현을 적으세요. Name : Date : Score : /26

01		형 놀라운	14		동 전달하다
02		명 발상	15		형 더러운
03		명 목소리	16		명 수영복
04		명 도움	17		형 신이 난
05		명 양말	18		명 공책
06		명 비밀	19		형 넓은
07		명 꼬리	20		형 줄이 쳐진
08		형 부드러운	21		명 뚜껑
09		동 타다	22		명 캐릭터
10		명 반지	23		명 머리카락
11		명 옷장	24		동 자르다
12		명 승리	25		명 미용사
13		명 선택	26		형 첫째의

정답 p.229

단어테스트 10

다음 한글 뜻을 보고 영어 표현을 적으세요. Name : Date : Score : /26

번호	답	뜻	번호	답	뜻
01		부 더 짧게	14		동 만나다
02		동 느끼다	15		명 비행
03		형 더 긴	16		명 이발
04		명 주의	17		명 선반
05		전 ~을 탑승하여	18		형 가득한
06		동 매다	19		명 위치
07		명 안전벨트	20		명 잠
08		명 안전	21		동 말하다
09		명 질문	22		동 놓다
10		명 직원	23		명 책
11		명 지우개	24		명 코치
12		동 부수다	25		명 표
13		명 기쁨	26		동 확인하다

정답 p.229

단어테스트 11

다음 한글 뜻을 보고 영어 표현을 적으세요. Name : Date : Score : /26

01		형 강한	14		부 아마
02		형 못생긴	15		명 악어
03		명 삼촌	16		명 부모
04		형 무서운	17		동 뛰다
05		명 사촌	18		형 늦은
06		명 장난감	19		형 눈이 내리는
07		명 총	20		형 먼
08		동 얻다, 받다	21		형 어두운
09		명 집	22		명 불
10		명 도넛	23		형 비가 오는
11		명 사탕	24		동 놀다
12		형 배고픈	25		부 밖에서
13		명 계란	26		명 쿠키

정답 p.229

단어테스트 12

다음 한글 뜻을 보고 영어 표현을 적으세요. Name : Date : Score : /26

01		㉻ 입다	
02		⑲ 재킷	
03		⑲ 겨울	
04		⑲ 봄	
05		㉻ 서두르다	
06		㉾ 이미	
07		⑲ 주인	
08		⑲ 천문관	
09		⑲ 장소	
10		㉳ 밝은	
11		㉾ 안에	
12		㉻ 보여주다	
13		⑲ 밤	
14		⑲ 별	
15		㉻ 발견하다	
16		⑲ 은하수	
17		⑲ 해(년)	
18		⑲ 주말	
19		㉾ 자주	
20		⑲ 사진	
21		⑲ 할아버지	
22		㉳ 흐린	
23		입다	
24		㉳ 진짜의	
25		㉳ 공통의	
26		⑲ 선택	

정답 p.229

단어테스트 13

다음 한글 뜻을 보고 영어 표현을 적으세요. Name : Date : Score : /26

01		㉑ 천재	14		㉑ 감옥
02		㉑ 스타	15		㉑ 아래층
03		㉑ 어른	16		㉑ 부엌
04		㉑ 우승자	17		㉑ 바구니
05		㉑ 승자	18		㉔ 수줍은
06		㉑ 용기, 통	19		㉑ 공원
07		㉑ 쌍둥이	20		㉔ 피곤한
08		㉑ 개	21		㉕ 일찍
09		㉑ 해파리	22		㉔ 게으른
10		㉔ 웃긴	23		㉔ 작동하지 않는
11		㉔ 무서워 하는	24		㉑ 알람
12		㉔ 작은	25		㉔ 늦은
13		㉑ 담임 선생님	26		㉑ 수업

정답 p.229

단어테스트 14

다음 한글 뜻을 보고 영어 표현을 적으세요. Name : Date : Score : /26

01		동 태워다 주다, 운전하다
02		명 학교
03		명 고향
04		형 키가 큰
05		형 똑똑한
06		형 못된
07		명 이웃
08		명 자리
09		형 목마른
10		명 디저트
11		명 냉장고
12		명 카페
13		형 완전 새 것인
14		명 만화
15		명 영화
16		형 최고의
17		부 혼자
18		형 더 나은
19		형 미친
20		형 스트레스를 받는
21		명 펭귄
22		명 회의
23		명 방문자
24		명 처음 온 사람
25		명 (특정 번호의) 전화
26		형 키가 작은

정답 p.229

워크북 정답

Dictation Test **1**

01. friends
02. four, fish
03. three, flowers
04. two, buses
05. a, deer
06. twins
07. friends
08. mistakes
09. two, foxes
10. three, mice

Dictation Test **2**

01. eyes
02. Children
03. babies
04. legs
05. glasses
06. a, cat
07. toes
08. socks
09. an, apple
10. a, table

Dictation Test **3**

01. America
02. English
03. math
04. Love
05. music
06. apple
07. glasses, juice
08. face
09. March
10. Saturday

Dictation Test **4**

01. lunch
02. sugar
03. water
04. Money
05. Meat
06. homework
07. Monday
08. piece, pizza
09. cup, coffee
10. from

Dictation Test **5**

01. a, student
02. an, umbrella
03. a, cake
04. a, doll
05. a, picture
06. a, present
07. an, artist
08. an, English
09. a, dog
10. a, bicycle

Dictation Test **6**

01. The, doll
02. The, moon
03. history
04. the, piano
05. lunch
06. The, apple
07. baseball
08. school
09. soccer
10. the, violin

Dictation Test **7**

01. I, walk
02. We, ride
03. She
04. You
05. He, me
06. us
07. I, her
08. I, want
09. them, him
10. He, me

Dictation Test **8**

01. He
02. She, it
03. She, them
04. we
05. I, it
06. You
07. it
08. me
09. him
10. us

Dictation Test **9**

01. our
02. your, friends
03. yours
04. his, hair
05. her, ruler
06. your, shoes
07. mine
08. his, bag
09. their
10. Its

Dictation Test **10**

01. hers
02. my, eraser
03. your, phone
04. his, room
05. our
06. theirs
07. his
08. hers
09. Their, teacher
10. ours

Dictation Test **11**

01. That, uncle
02. This
03. It, cold
04. It
05. Those
06. These, books
07. these, photos
08. day, it
09. This
10. that, book

Dictation Test **12**

01. those, animals
02. It
03. That
04. These
05. those, flowers
06. It
07. This, dad
08. It, dark
09. That
10. time, it

Dictation Test **13**

01. dad, is
02. She, is
03. I, am
04. hobby, is
05. mother, is
06. kids, are
07. You, are
08. I, am
09. We, are
10. He, is

Dictation Test **14**

01. They, are
02. is
03. I, am
04. is
05. is
06. They, are
07. You, are
08. We, are
09. is
10. He, is

단어테스트 1

01. teacher
02. student
03. boy
04. girl
05. friend
06. park
07. school
08. month
09. year
10. room
11. house
12. brother
13. store
14. book
15. umbrella
16. flower
17. scissors
18. glasses
19. pants
20. dish
21. church
22. story
23. lady
24. leaf
25. foot
26. sheep

단어테스트 2

01. wash
02. eraser
03. computer
04. onion
05. sofa
06. classroom
07. wear
08. catch
09. river
10. miss
11. refrigerator
12. yesterday
13. eat
14. playground
15. snowball fight
16. lend
17. weekend
18. errand
19. chocolate
20. born
21. artist
22. see
23. zoo
24. butterfly
25. present
26. really

단어테스트 3

01. math
02. like
03. love
04. soccer
05. thirsty
06. need
07. drink
08. refrigerator
09. basket
10. room
11. eat
12. dinner
13. furniture
14. pants
15. chair
16. paper
17. desk
18. sheet
19. round
20. birthday
21. basketball
22. usually
23. listen
24. make
25. lunch
26. flour

단어테스트 4

01. sugar
02. look
03. smoke
04. burn
05. again
06. oil
07. pee

워크북 정답

08. government
09. nature
10. knowledge
11. desire
12. friendship
13. sum
14. success
15. let
16. sense
17. fear
18. sunshine
19. vegetable
20. plant
21. shade
22. dream
23. homework
24. help
25. situation
26. hope

단어테스트 5

01. shiny
02. give
03. delicious
04. together
05. bright
06. see
07. picture
08. young
09. worry
10. duty
11. cute
12. shy
13. live
14. buy
15. pretty
16. want
17. present
18. cold
19. muffler
20. coat
21. lose
22. rise
23. night
24. beautiful
25. sky
26. fight

단어테스트 6

01. bathroom
02. before
03. wear
04. blind
05. bat
06. glasses
07. cap
08. suitcase
09. kind
10. left
11. summer
12. awake
13. pet
14. speak
15. advice
16. judge
17. dream
18. heart
19. artist
20. neighbor
21. priceless
22. treasure
23. ground
24. late
25. crosswalk
26. joke

단어테스트 7

01. awesome
02. fever
03. mess
04. buy
05. cook
06. friend
07. classmate
08. lovely
09. son
10. remember
11. forget
12. hate
13. lend
14. exercise
15. pajama
16. invite
17. movie
18. taste
19. wait
20. selfish
21. colored
22. pencil
23. share
24. ask
25. sharpener
26. fan

단어테스트 8

01. watch
02. hope
03. sing
04. tone-deaf
05. carry
06. tune
07. singer
08. envy
09. turn
10. give
11. stuffed
12. fluffy
13. name
14. draw
15. tomorrow
16. map
17. teenager
18. know
19. think
20. speak
21. fair
22. pursue
23. courage
24. wonderful
25. bake
26. call

단어테스트 9

01. amazing
02. idea
03. voice
04. help
05. socks
06. secret
07. tail
08. soft
09. ride
10. ring
11. closet
12. victory
13. choice
14. pass
15. dirty
16. swimsuit
17. excited
18. notebook
19. wide
20. ruled
21. cap
22. character
23. hair
24. cut
25. hairdresser
26. first

단어테스트 10

01. shorter
02. feel
03. longer
04. attention
05. aboard
06. fasten
07. seat belt
08. safety
09. question
10. staff
11. eraser
12. break
13. pleasure
14. meet
15. flight
16. haircut
17. tray
18. full
19. position
20. sleep
21. talk
22. put
23. book
24. coach
25. ticket
26. check

단어테스트 11

01. strong
02. ugly
03. uncle
04. afraid
05. cousin
06. toy
07. gun
08. get
09. house
10. doughnut
11. candy
12. hungry
13. egg
14. maybe
15. crocodile
16. parents
17. run
18. late
19. snowy
20. far
21. dark
22. light
23. rainy
24. play
25. outside
26. cookie

단어테스트 12

01. wear
02. jacket
03. winter
04. spring
05. hurry
06. already
07. owner
08. planetarium
09. place
10. bright
11. inside
12. show
13. night
14. star
15. find
16. milky way
17. year
18. weekend
19. often
20. photo
21. grandfather
22. cloudy
23. put on
24. real
25. common
26. choice

단어테스트 13

01. genius
02. star
03. grown-up
04. champion
05. winner
06. case
07. twins
08. dog
09. jellyfish
10. funny
11. scared
12. small
13. homeroom teacher
14. jail
15. downstairs
16. kitchen
17. basket
18. shy
19. park
20. tired
21. early
22. lazy
23. dead
24. alarm
25. late
26. class

단어테스트 14

01. drive
02. school
03. hometown
04. tall
05. clever
06. mean
07. neighbor

08. seat
09. thirsty
10. dessert
11. fridge
12. cafe
13. brand new
14. cartoon
15. movie
16. best
17. alone
18. better
19. mad
20. stressed
21. penguin
22. meeting
23. visitor
24. stranger
25. line
26. short

정답 p. 12

TEST 핵심 문법 사항

인칭대명사

TEST 1

다음 빈칸에 알맞은 인칭대명사를 쓰세요.

수	인칭	주격	소유격	목적격	소유대명사
단수	1	I	❶	me	❷
	2	❸	your	you	❹
	3	he	his	❺	❻
		she	her	❼	hers
		it	❽	it	
복수	1	we	our	❾	ours
	2	❿	your	⓫	yours
	3	they	their	⓬	theirs

TEST 2

다음 괄호에서 어법상 알맞은 단어를 고르세요.

1 The old man asked my sister (me, my) address.

2 Where does (he, his) live?

3 Every day has (it, its) own meaning.

4 I like (his, him) very much.

5 I have a dog. (Its, It's) name is Spot.

TEST 3

다음을 인칭대명사(he, she, it, we, you, they)로 바꾸어 쓰세요.

1 Tom and Jane ➡ ______________

2 you and your teacher ➡ ______________

3 a tall man ➡ ______________

4 that pretty girl ➡ ______________

5 his bag ➡ ______________

6 you and I ➡ ______________

정답 p. 12

명사의 복수형

TEST 4

다음 빈칸에 알맞은 내용을 쓰세요.

1 규칙 복수형 I

경우	규칙	단어 예시
대부분의 경우	-s	pencil - pencils, sport - sports
-s, -x, -ch, -sh로 끝날 때	❶ ______	bus - ❷ ______, box - ❸ ______, church - ❹ ______, dish - ❺ ______
자음 +o로 끝날 때	❻ ______	potato - ❼ ______, tomato - ❽ ______ ***cf.*** piano - ❾ ______, photo - ❿ ______
모음 +o로 끝날 때	⓫ ______	radio - ⓬ ______, audio - ⓭ ______

2 규칙 복수형 II

경우	규칙	단어 예시
자음+y로 끝날 때	y를 ❶ ______ 로 바꾸고 ❷ ______	candy - ❸ ______, country - ❹ ______
모음+y로 끝날 때	❺ ______	day - ❻ ______, boy - ❼ ______
-f, -fe로 끝날 때	f / fe를 ❽ ______ 로 바꾸고 ❾ ______	leaf - ❿ ______, wolf - ⓫ ______ knife - ⓬ ______ ***cf.*** roof - ⓭ ______

3 불규칙 복수형

경우	단어 예시
단수형과 복수형이 같은 명사	deer - ❶ ______, fish - ❷ ______, sheep - ❸ ______
그 밖의 명사의 불규칙 복수형	foot - ❹ ______, tooth - ❺ ______, man - ❻ ______, woman - ❼ ______, goose - ❽ ______, mouse - ❾ ______

정답은 뒷면에서 확인하세요.

Circle and write.

알맞은 것에 동그라미 하고 빈칸에 쓰세요.

1.

et　en　ed

b e d

2.

et　en　ed

j ___ ___

3.

et　en　ed

p ___ ___

4.

et　en　ed

r ___ ___

5.

et　en　ed

v ___ ___

6.

et　en　ed

t ___ ___

Circle and write.

알맞은 것에 동그라미 하고 빈칸에 쓰세요.

1\.

et en ed

b e d

2\.

et en ed

j e t

3\.

et en ed

p e n

4\.

et en ed

r e d

5\.

et en ed

v e t

6\.

et en ed

t e n

초등영문법 3800제

정답과 해설

입문 1단계 명사/관사/대명사/be동사

1

LEVEL

MOTHERTONGUE
마더텅출판사
since1999.4.1.

초등영문법 3800제

정답과 해설

입문 1단계

1 LEVEL

Chapter 01 명사

Unit 01 셀 수 있는 명사

Check and Write

▶ 본문 p.9

A 2. pencil
I have a pencil. 나는 연필 한 자루를 가지고 있다.

B 2. an, umbrella
You need an umbrella when it rains.
비가 올 때 너는 우산이 필요하다.

C 2. an, apple

Unit 02 명사의 복수형

Check and Write

▶ 본문 p.11

2. dishes
They are washing the dishes. 그들은 설거지를 하고 있다.
3. potatoes
The baby has many potatoes. 아기는 감자를 많이 갖고 있다.

Practice 1

▶ 본문 p.12

A 2. an, eraser 3. scissors 4. a, computer 5. a, book

B 1. an, egg 2. apples 3. bananas 4. an, onion 5. tomatoes

C 1. a, table 2. flowers 3. a, sofa 4. a, cat 5. a, clock

D 1. students 2. glasses 3. fish 4. buses 5. friends

Practice 2

▶ 본문 p.14

2. Dad ate an apple this morning
아빠는 오늘 아침에 사과 한 개를 드셨다.
3. It has snowed for three days
3일 동안 눈이 내렸다.
4. There are many children on the playground for a snowball fight
눈싸움을 하기 위해 운동장에 많은 아이들이 있다.
5. His feet sank into the snow
그의 두 발이 눈 속에 빠졌다.
6. I have two umbrellas in the classroom
나 교실에 우산 두 개 있어!
7. Do you want me to lend you an umbrella
내가 우산 한 개 빌려 줄까?
8. My socks are wet
내 양말이 젖었어!
9. There are seven days in a week
한 주에는 7일이 있다.
10. I sleep for 10 hours a day on weekends
나는 주말엔 하루에 10시간 동안 자.
11. Will you run an errand for me, please
나를 위해 심부름 하나 해주겠니?
12. Would you put these two boxes out
이 상자 두 개를 밖에 버려줄래?
13. Can you sweep the fallen leaves in the yard
마당에 있는 낙엽들을 쓸어줄래?
14. Please tell me some fun stories
나에게 재미있는 이야기들을 들려줘.
15. Brush your teeth after eating chocolate
초콜릿을 먹고 나서 이를 닦아!
16. All men must choose between two paths
모든 사람들은 두 가지 길 중에 하나를 골라야 해.
17. Fish are friends
18. We all make mistakes
우리는 모두 실수(들)를 한다.
19. All children are born artists
모든 아이들은 타고난 예술가이다.
20. All our dreams can come true

Practice 3

▶ 본문 p.17

2. They are twins
그들은 쌍둥이야.
3. I see two wolves at the zoo
나는 동물원에서 늑대 두 마리를 본다.
4. They are two foxes, not wolves
그것들은 여우 두 마리지, 늑대들이 아니야.
5. I saw three mice
나 쥐 세 마리 봤어!
6. There are five deer in the forest
숲에 사슴 다섯 마리가 있어.
7. I see many butterflies in the countryside
나는 시골에서 많은 나비들을 본다.
8. Look at the two babies
저기 아기 두 명 좀 봐!
9. Children run in the park
공원에서 아이들이 뛴다.
10. There are three women in my house
11. I have a present for you
너를 위한 선물 하나가 있어.
12. It has really short legs
그것은 진짜 짧은 다리를 가졌어!
13. There is an orange in the refrigerator
냉장고에 오렌지 하나가 있어.
14. Close your eyes
눈을 감아 봐.
15. I don't feel my toes
내 발가락들이 느껴지지 않아(내 발가락들에 감각이 없어).
16. I finally got a cat
나 결국 고양이 한 마리 생겼어!
17. It peed on my pants
그게 내 바지 위에 오줌 쌌어.
18. I need a pair of pants and two pairs of shoes
저는 바지 한 벌과 신발 두 켤레가 필요해요.
19. Captain America and Iron Man are my favorite heroes
캡틴 아메리카와 아이언 맨은 내가 가장 좋아하는 영웅들이야!
20. I wear glasses
나는 안경을 쓴다.

Let's Practice More!

SET 01
▶ 본문 p.20

02. a, computer
03. a, book
04. an, eraser
05. a, banana
06. a, table
07. a, tomato
08. a, flower
09. an, egg
10. a, cat
11. a, sofa
12. a, clock

SET 02
▶ 본문 p.21

02. a, student
03. a, fish
04. a, bus
05. an, errand
06. a, wolf
07. a, good, day
08. an, umbrella
09. a, box
10. a, story
11. a, bad, tooth
12. a, mistake
13. a, gift
14. an, onion

SET 03
▶ 본문 p.22

02. a, hero
03. a, mouse
04. an, older, sister
05. a, butterfly
06. a, woman
07. an, orange
08. a, present
09. a, kid
10. a, baby
11. a, police, officer
12. a, dream
13. an, hour
14. an, eye

SET 04
▶ 본문 p.23

02. (m)ice
03. (b)ooks
04. (f)lowers
05. (g)lasses
06. (b)uses
07. (f)riends
08. (s)cissors
09. (s)tudents
10. (d)ays
11. (c)hildren
12. (a)pples

SET 05
▶ 본문 p.24

02. (u)mbrellas
03. (s)ocks
04. (c)hildren
05. (d)ays
06. (h)ours
07. (b)oxes
08. (s)tories
09. (l)eaves
10. (t)eeth
11. (m)istakes
12. (d)reams
13. (w)olves
14. (f)oxes

SET 06
▶ 본문 p.25

02. (b)utterflies
03. (b)abies
04. (t)wins
05. (C)hildren
06. (w)omen
07. (o)ranges
08. (e)yes
09. (t)oes
10. (l)egs
11. (f)igures
12. (k)nives
13. (c)ats
14. (h)eroes

SET 07
▶ 본문 p.26

02. A, monkey, banana
03. a, hero
04. babies, twins
05. leaves
06. three, cats
07. deer
08. a, pencil
09. scissors
10. an, onion
11. many, flowers
12. five, students
13. a, kid[child]
14. a, friend
15. eight, hours
16. feet
17. an, umbrella
18. days, a
19. two, fish
20. stories

SET 08
▶ 본문 p.28

02. children
03. two, oranges
04. butterflies
05. toes
06. two, apples
07. an, eraser
08. teeth
09. mistakes
10. dreams
11. two, wolves
12. Three, mice
13. hours, a
14. a, present[gift]
15. a, box, cats
16. short, legs
17. three, pencils
18. a, sofa
19. four, dogs
20. an, errand

Unit 03 셀 수 없는 명사

Check and Write
▶ 본문 p.31

A paper, water
B Busan, London, December, Korea

Unit 04 셀 수 없는 명사의 수량표현

Check and Write
▶ 본문 p.33

two glasses of, two slices of, a cup of, a bar of, a piece of

Practice 1
▶ 본문 p.34

A 2. English 3. math 4. Monday, Sihu 5. Love
B 1. soccer 2. water 3. water 4. juice 5. glasses
C 1. apple 2. bread 3. chocolate 4. pizza 5. pig
D 1. furniture 2. pants 3. money 4. paper 5. work

Practice 2
▶ 본문 p.36

2. My birthday is in March
내 생일은 3월이야.
3. My birthday is in February
내 생일은 2월이야.
4. I like Saturday best
나는 토요일을 가장 좋아해.
5. play basketball on Saturday
6. interest in student government
7. with mom on Sunday
8. desire knowledge
9. We need a lot of sugar
10. Look at the smoke
11. Your mom burned the food
12. more oil in the pan
13. spilled water on your smartphone
14. It is not water
그거 물 아니야.
15. listen to music on Sunday
16. flour and milk
17. They play soccer
18. Success is the sum
19. Money is not everything
돈이 전부인 것은 아니야.
20. I sense much fear

Practice 3
▶ 본문 p.39

2. juice
Three bottles of juice are on the table
세 병의 주스가 탁자 위에 있어.
3. Bread
Bread comes from plants
빵은 식물들에서 유래한다.

4. Milk
Milk comes from animals
우유는 동물들에서 유래한다.

5. Meat
Meat comes from animals
고기는 동물들에서 유래한다.

6. snow
We had snow in April this year
올해에는 4월에 눈이 왔었다.

7. shade
Let's make some shade for the baby
아기를 위해 그늘을 만들자!

8. sun
The sun rises in the east
태양은 동쪽에서 뜬다.

9. love
"Romeo and Juliet" is a story about love
'로미오와 줄리엣'은 사랑에 대한 이야기야.

10. homework
I have a lot of homework to do
나는 해야 할 숙제가 많아.

11. help
Good friends will give you help in bad situations
좋은 친구는 나쁜 상황에서 너에게 도움을 줄 것이다.

12. hope
but there is still hope

13. information
That is totally new information
그것은 완전히 새로운 정보구나!

14. paper
Wasn't there just a sheet of paper
그저 종이 한 장만 있지 않았어?

15. health
Drinking much soft drink is not good for your health
탄산음료를 많이 마시는 것은 너의 건강에 좋지 않아.

16. plastic
We should recycle plastic to save the environment
우리는 환경을 구하기 위해 플라스틱을 재활용해야 해.

17. Friendship
Friendship is important to me
우정은 나에게 중요해.

18. sheets
The test was made up of two sheets of paper
시험은 종이 두 장으로 이루어져 있었어.

19. loaves, cup[glass]
I eat two loaves of bread and drink a cup[glass] of milk for breakfast
나는 아침식사로 빵 두 덩어리와 우유 한 컵을 마셔.

Let's Practice More!

SET 01
▶ 본문 p.42

02. love 03. juice
04. English, math 05. bread 06. work
07. hair 08. Monday 09. April
10. cheese, flour 11. money 12. success

SET 02
▶ 본문 p.43

02. Mina, America 03. oil
04. Junwoo, Saturday 05. milk
06. Money 07. sugar, salt 08. furniture
09. interest 10. Friendship
11. (The) sun, (the) east 12. snow
13. courage 14. homework

SET 03
▶ 본문 p.44

02. Sunshine 03. confidence 04. paper
05. advice 06. information
07. hope, success 08. health 09. smoke
10. bread, milk 11. Meat 12. February
13. peace 14. paper

SET 04
▶ 본문 p.45

02. (l)oaf 03. (g)lass 04. (s)heets
05. (g)lasses 06. (p)iece 07. (b)ottles
08. (p)iece 09. (s)lices 10. (b)ottle 11. (b)ars
12. (l)oaves

SET 05
▶ 본문 p.46

02. (c)up 03. (b)ar 04. (g)lass
05. (l)oaves 06. (s)heets 07. (p)ieces 08. (b)ars
09. (s)heet 10. (l)oaf 11. (b)ottles
12. (p)ieces 13. (g)lasses 14. (c)ups

SET 06
▶ 본문 p.47

02. (g)lasses 03. (b)ottles 04. (b)ar
05. (c)ups 06. (s)heets 07. (g)lasses
08. (b)ottles 09. (p)ieces 10. (p)iece 11. (l)oaf
12. (g)lass 13. (p)ieces 14. (c)up

SET 07
▶ 본문 p.48

02. pieces[slices], pizza 03. Friendship
04. glass[cup], water 05. Money
06. piece[slice], cheese 07. money
08. bottles, juice 09. glass, milk
10. work 11. bars, chocolate
12. information 13. flour, milk
14. March 15. bottle, juice
16. sheets, paper 17. water
18. loaves, bread 19. English, math
20. glasses, juice

SET 08
▶ 본문 p.50

02. cup, coffee 03. bottle, oil
04. sheets, paper 05. pieces[slices], cake
06. math 07. piece[slice], cheese
08. oil 09. bar, chocolate
10. bottles, wine 11. bars, soap
12. glass, wine 13. love
14. loaf, bread 15. birthday
16. interest 17. sugar
18. pieces[slices], cheese 19. health
20. bars, chocolate

Chapter 02 관사

Unit 01 부정관사

Check and Write

▶ 본문 p.55

2. a	3. an	4. an	5. a
6. a	7. x	8. an	9. x
10. an	11. a	12. x	

Unit 02 정관사

Check and Write

▶ 본문 p.57

2. The	3. a	4. The	5. the
6. x	7. x	8. The	

Practice 1

▶ 본문 p.58

A 2. The, picture 3. a, student
4. x, math, x, English 5. the, piano

B 1. a, dog 2. The, dog 3. a, cat
4. The, cat 5. x, family

C 1. a, cake 2. a, doll 3. The, doll
4. a, necklace 5. a, hair, clip

D 1. an, umbrella 2. an, umbrella
3. the, umbrella
4. a, muffler, a, coat 5. x, muffler

Practice 2

▶ 본문 p.60

2. the sky	3. the sun, the moon
4. home	5. school
6. breakfast	7. a bat
8. The hat	9. a girl, The girl
10. the left	11. chocolate
12. Busan	13. an apple, The apple
14. The sky	15. A pet
16. A hero, the world	17. A dog
18. A dream, a wish	19. an artist
20. A good neighbor	

Practice 3

▶ 본문 p.63

2. the piano
You cannot play the piano
너 피아노 칠 줄 모르잖아.

3. the window
Look out the window
창문 밖을 봐.

4. an umbrella
I don't have an umbrella
나 우산 없는데!

5. an umbrella
Do you have an umbrella
너 우산 있니?

6. The sun
The sun does not shine
해가 빛나지 않아.

7. school
I run to school

8. an accident
There was an accident at the crosswalk
횡단보도에서 어떤 사고가 났다.

9. the violin
Can you play the violin
너 바이올린을 연주할 수 있니?

10. a problem
I have a problem with my computer
내 컴퓨터에 어떤 문제가 있어.

11. a joke
I heard a joke today
나 오늘 농담 하나를 들었어.

12. The joke
The joke was very funny
그 농담은 매우 재미있었어.

13. lunch
I had lunch yesterday
어제 나는 점심을 먹었다.

14. soccer
He often plays soccer
그는 종종 축구를 한다.

15. home
Mina goes home early because she has a cold
미나는 감기에 걸렸기 때문에 일찍 집에 간다.

16. A dog
A dog doesn't try to give advice or judge you
개는 너에게 조언을 하거나 너를 판단하려고 하지 않아.

17. A pet
A pet is a good friend
애완동물은 좋은 친구이다.

18. The bike
The bike is really cool
그 자전거는 정말 멋지다.

19. a present[gift]
I have a present[gift] for you
나 너한테 줄 선물이 하나 있어.

20. The gloves
The gloves are very warm
그 장갑은 매우 따뜻하다.

Let's Practice More!

SET 01

▶ 본문 p.66

02. an	03. x	04. an	05. an
06. a	07. a	08. a	09. x
10. A	11. x	12. a	

SET 02

▶ 본문 p.67

02. A	03. an	04. an	05. an
06. An	07. a	08. an	09. x
10. a	11. an	12. a	13. an
14. a, a			

SET 03

▶ 본문 p.68

02. A	03. a	04. an	05. a

06. x
07. a
08. a
09. A
10. x
11. an
12. x
13. an
14. a

SET 04

▶ 본문 p.69

02. The
03. x
04. x
05. The
06. the
07. The
08. x
09. The
10. x
11. the
12. x

SET 05

▶ 본문 p.70

02. the
03. The
04. x
05. The
06. the
07. The
08. the
09. the
10. x
11. the
12. the
13. The
14. The

SET 06

▶ 본문 p.71

02. the, the
03. x
04. The
05. x
06. The
07. x
08. the
09. x
10. The
11. x
12. the
13. The
14. the

SET 07

▶ 본문 p.72

02. A, good, friend
03. lunch
04. the, piano
05. an, honest, boy
06. The, book
07. A, dog
08. home
09. The, trip
10. The, computer
11. the
12. an, accident
13. the, sun, the, moon
14. a, joke
15. money
16. friend
17. an, umbrella
18. a, doctor
19. the, west
20. school

SET 08

▶ 본문 p.74

02. The, boy
03. books
04. a, picture
05. the, picture
06. a, muffler
07. an, eraser
08. the, umbrella
09. a, present
10. The, present
11. A, dream
12. the, dream
13. an, umbrella
14. An, apple
15. The, apple
16. an, artist
17. The, artist
18. a, student
19. a, dog
20. The, dog

Chapter 01~02 실전테스트

▶ 본문 p.76

01. pen, tree
02. s, h
03. e, e
04. v, e, s
05. bar
06. loaf
07. piece
08. cup
09. sheets
10. love (추상명사)
11. apple (가산명사)
12. 셀 수 있는 명사 - family, team, tree
    셀 수 없는 명사 - milk, love, USA, bread
13. 셀 수 있는 명사 - flower, egg
    셀 수 없는 명사 - water, hope, juice
14. He has five dishes.
15. I want three boxes.
16. Children hold their hands.
17. an
18. the
19. a
20. a
21. the
22. The
23. an
24. James reads a[the] book.
25. She has two children.
26. I play the piano on Monday.
27. My father eats three tomatoes.
28. Do you like fish?
29. 잘못 쓴 부분 : ③ 고쳐 쓰기 : the
30. 잘못 쓴 부분 : ① 고쳐 쓰기 : The

Chapter 03 인칭대명사

Unit 01 주격 인칭대명사

Check and Write

▶ 본문 p.83

2. She
3. They
4. I
5. You
6. We
7. You

Unit 02 목적격 인칭대명사

Check and Write

▶ 본문 p.85

2. her
3. them
4. us
5. you
6. me

Practice 1

▶ 본문 p.86

A 2. I 3. They 4. We 5. me 6. it

B 1. me 2. he, them 3. them, him 4. him 5. it 6. He

C 1. she 2. She, it 3. She, it 4. her 5. she, them

D 1. you 2. I 3. Me

Practice 2

▶ 본문 p.88

2. I envy her
   난 그녀가 부러워.
3. I am turning thirteen
   나는 13살이 된다!
4. They are my best friends
   그들은 나의 가장 친한 친구들이다.
5. Jinho gives me a stuffed cat
   진호는 나에게 고양이 인형을 준다.
6. It was so fluffy
   그것은 매우 보송보송했다.
7. I named it "Meow"
   나는 그것에게 '야옹이'라고 이름을 지어주었다.

8. Sihu gives me colored pencils
시후는 나에게 색연필들을 준다.
9. I will draw "Meow" with them
나는 그것들로 '야옹이'를 그릴 것이다.
10. we had a chocolate cake
11. It was really delicious
그것은 정말 맛있었다.
12. eat it again tomorrow
13. They are not really your friends
그들은 진짜 너의 친구들이 아니야.
14. It is out there
그건 저 밖에 있어.
15. you must do it yourself
16. they know everything
17. the world will speak for him
18. we go beyond them
19. Get used to it
그것에 익숙해져라.
20. We have the courage to pursue it
우린 그것을 좇으려는 용기가 있다.

Practice 3

▶ 본문 p.91

2. I want to be like her
나는 그녀처럼 되고 싶어.
3. I want to get something special for him
나는 그를 위해 특별한 무언가를 주고 싶다.
4. He loves "Kung Fu Panda"
그는 '쿵푸팬더'를 정말 좋아한다.
5. I will give him a stuffed panda
[I will give a stuffed panda to him]
나는 그에게 판다 인형을 줄 것이다.
6. he likes it
7. My mom bakes cookies for me
우리 엄마는 나를 위해 쿠키를 구우신다.
8. I called my best friend, Mina
나는 나의 가장 친한 친구인 미나에게 전화했다.
9. They smell delicious
그것들은 맛있는 냄새가 난다.
10. Share them with me
나랑 그것들을 나눠먹자.
11. We have them together
우리는 함께 그것들을 먹는다.
12. I packed them for her brother
나는 그녀의 남동생을 위해 그것들을 싸 주었다.
13. She does not allow me to play mobile games
그녀는 내가 모바일 게임을 하지 못하게 한다.
14. it is fair
15. I will play with my smartphone
16. Suho treats me differently
수호는 나를 다르게 대한다.
17. She watches a TV series every night
그녀는 매일 밤 텔레비전 연속물을 본다.
18. he loves me
19. the world will speak for him
20. we have the courage to pursue them

Let's Practice More!

SET 01

▶ 본문 p.94

02. I	03. We	04. We	05. I
06. We	07. I	08. I	09. We
10. We	11. I	12. I	

SET 02

▶ 본문 p.95

02. 단수	03. 복수	04. 단수	05. 복수
06. 복수	07. 단수	08. 복수	09. 단수
10. 단수	11. 복수	12. 단수	13. 복수
14. 단수			

SET 03

▶ 본문 p.96

02. She	03. It	04. He	05. They
06. She	07. It	08. He	09. She
10. They	11. He	12. It	13. She
14. They			

SET 04

▶ 본문 p.97

02. me	03. me	04. us	05. me
06. us	07. me	08. us	09. us
10. me	11. me	12. us	

SET 05

▶ 본문 p.98

02. 복수	03. 단수	04. 복수	05. 단수
06. 단수	07. 단수	08. 복수	09. 단수
10. 복수	11. 복수	12. 복수	13. 단수
14. 복수			

SET 06

▶ 본문 p.99

02. it	03. her	04. them	05. her
06. him	07. it	08. it	09. them
10. her	11. him	12. them	13. it
14. her			

SET 07

▶ 본문 p.100

02. She	03. me	04. I, them
05. He	06. We, her	07. They
08. I, her	09. him	10. They, they
11. He, them	12. She	13. It
14. She, us	15. It	16. We, you
17. You	18. They, me	19. I, it
20. He, us		

SET 08

▶ 본문 p.101

02. I, you	03. I, he	04. They
05. She	06. They	07. them, me
08. He	09. You, they	10. We, them
11. I, it	12. she	13. He, us
14. They, you	15. me	16. It
17. We	18. her	19. She
20. us		

Unit 03 소유격 인칭대명사

Check and Write

▶ 본문 p.103

2. their	3. my	4. our
5. Its	6. his	

Unit 04 소유대명사

Check and Write
▶ 본문 p.105

2. yours 3. hers 4. Theirs
5. yours 6. his

Practice 1
▶ 본문 p.106

A 2. Yours 3. yours 4. mine 5. my
6. yours 7. mine
B 1. my 2. his 3. his 4. his
5. Its
C 1. her 2. his 3. her 4. hers
D 1. your 2. our 3. your, your 4. our

Practice 2
▶ 본문 p.108

2. his 3. your 4. yours
5. Mine 6. his 7. my
8. yours 9. our 10. your
11. your 12. their 13. my
14. her 15. yours 16. Our
17. my 18. hers 19. our
20. her

Practice 3
▶ 본문 p.111

2. check my ticket
3. My seat number is 7B
4. your car number is
5. borrow your scissors
6. What's wrong with yours
네 것은 뭔가 잘못됐니?
7. My brother took mine
내 형이 내 것을 가져갔어.
8. like your new look
9. my hairdresser cut it too short
10. It is better than mine
그건 내 것보다 나아.
11. My sister and I went shopping
내 여동생과 나는 쇼핑을 갔다.
12. check her shopping list
13. liked her Hello Kitty ruler
14. mine is longer than hers
15. she always borrows mine
16. bought our notebooks
17. are different from mine
18. taking a nap in his room
19. someone else's needs before yours
20. Their teacher teaches math
그들의 선생님은 수학을 가르치신다.

Let's Practice More!

SET 01
▶ 본문 p.114

02. our 03. our 04. their
05. your 06. their 07. My
08. Our 09. her 10. her
11. our 12. her

SET 02
▶ 본문 p.115

02. your 03. his 04. her
05. your 06. our 07. My
08. their 09. his 10. your
11. her 12. their 13. your
14. Their

SET 03
▶ 본문 p.116

02. her 03. Our 04. Your
05. my 06. my 07. my
08. Your 09. Its 10. my
11. her 12. his 13. our
14. his

SET 04
▶ 본문 p.117

02. his 03. yours 04. ours
05. his 06. mine 07. his
08. theirs 09. Ours 10. Hers
11. his 12. Theirs

SET 05
▶ 본문 p.118

02. hers 03. mine 04. his
05. ours 06. mine 07. yours
08. hers 09. mine 10. Ours
11. Yours 12. his 13. hers
14. yours

SET 06
▶ 본문 p.119

02. hers 03. hers 04. yours
05. Yours 06. yours 07. ours
08. hers 09. ours 10. Theirs
11. Yours 12. his 13. hers
14. theirs

SET 07
▶ 본문 p.120

02. A 03. A 04. A 05. B
06. A 07. B 08. A 09. A
10. B 11. A 12. B 13. A
14. B 15. A 16. A 17. B
18. A 19. A 20. A

SET 08
▶ 본문 p.122

02. your, scissors 03. His, notebooks
04. theirs 05. my, seat
06. Your 07. hers
08. his 09. our
10. my, new, haircut 11. ours
12. hers 13. Your, seat, number
14. our 15. yours
16. Your 17. Our
18. Yours 19. Theirs
20. his, hair

Chapter 04 지시대명사와 비인칭주어 it

Unit 01 지시대명사 this, these / that, those / it

Check and Write

▶ 본문 p.127

2. it	3. This	4. That
5. these	6. Those	7. it

Unit 02 지시형용사 / 비인칭주어 it

Check and Write

▶ 본문 p.129

2. These	3. It	4. It
5. that	6. those	7. It

Practice 1

▶ 본문 p.130

A	2. It	3. It	4. That	5. those
	6. that[those]	7. it[that]	8. It[That]	9. those
B	1. this, this	2. That	3. that	
C	1. this	2. It	3. It	4. it
D	1. it	2. It	3. it	4. it

Practice 2

▶ 본문 p.132

2. the name of that star
3. It is so bright
그건 정말 밝아요.
4. That is called Sirius
저것은 시리우스라고 불려.
5. It is a bright star
그것은 밝은 별이야.
6. It is Christmas Eve
크리스마스이브다.
7. It is six thirty
여섯 시 삼십 분이다.
8. It is already dark
벌써 어둡다.
9. These books are mine
이 책들은 내 것이다.
10. It would be a white Christmas
화이트 크리스마스가 될 거야.(크리스마스에 눈이 올 거야.)
11. Let it snow
눈이 내리게 해 주세요!
12. It snowed yesterday
어제는 눈이 내렸다.
13. It is cloudy
날씨가 흐리다.
14. all these things
15. When it rains
16. This is the real world
이건 실제 세상이야!
17. It is dark and rainy
어둡고 비가 내리고 있다.
18. That's another thing
19. That's a bad choice
그것은 나쁜 선택이다.
20. It is too late
너무 늦었어.

Practice 3

▶ 본문 p.134

2. It looks old
그건 낡아 보여요.
3. That is your father's diary
저건 네 아버지의 일기장이야.
4. Where did you find it
그것을 어디에서 찾았니?
5. It was between those books
저 책들 사이에 있었어요.
6. What time is it
몇 시예요?
7. It is 7 o'clock
일곱 시 정각이야.
8. Is it cold today
오늘 추워요?
9. It is cold and windy
춥고 바람이 불어.
10. it snows this Christmas
11. it is sunny
12. That is why I am sad
그것이 내가 슬픈 이유이다.
13. Let it snow
눈이 내리게 해 주세요!
14. it is broken
15. It is very hot today
오늘은 매우 더워.
16. It will be fixed
17. We will play soccer this weekend
우리는 이번 주말에 축구를 할 것이다.
18. I agree with that idea
나는 저 생각에 동의한다.
19. It snowed yesterday
어제는 눈이 왔다.
20. This is the real world
이건 실제 세상이야!

Let's Practice More!

SET 01

▶ 본문 p.136

02. That	03. That	04. This	05. That
06. That	07. That	08. This	09. This
10. That	11. This	12. That	

SET 02

▶ 본문 p.137

02. This	03. These	04. This	05. This
06. These	07. This	08. These	09. This
10. These	11. These	12. This	13. These
14. This			

SET 03

▶ 본문 p.138

02. That	03. Those	04. That	05. Those
06. That	07. That	08. Those	09. Those
10. That	11. Those	12. That	13. Those
14. Those			

SET 04
▶ 본문 p.139

02. this 03. these 04. These 05. this
06. these 07. This 08. this 09. these
10. this 11. This 12. this

SET 05
▶ 본문 p.140

02. that 03. those 04. That 05. that
06. those 07. that 08. That 09. those
10. That 11. That 12. that 13. Those
14. that

SET 06
▶ 본문 p.141

02. 형 03. 대 04. 대 05. 형
06. 대 07. 형 08. 대 09. 형
10. 대 11. 형 12. 형 13. 대
14. 대

SET 07
▶ 본문 p.142

02. 비 03. 지 04. 비 05. 비
06. 지 07. 지 08. 지 09. 비
10. 지 11. 지 12. 비 13. 비
14. 지 15. 지 16. 비 17. 비
18. 비 19. 지 20. 비

SET 08
▶ 본문 p.144

02. It 03. It 04. Those 05. That
06. that 07. These 08. those 09. this
10. it 11. That 12. It 13. this
14. These 15. These 16. those 17. That
18. These 19. This 20. these

Chapter 05 be동사

Unit 01 주어에 따라 다른 be동사

Check and Write
▶ 본문 p.149

2. are 3. is 4. am
5. are 6. is

Unit 02 be동사의 우리말 뜻

Check and Write
▶ 본문 p.151

A 2. ~에 있다 3. ~이다 4. ~에 있다

B 2. She's shy.
3. They're in the amusement park.

Practice 1
▶ 본문 p.152

A 2. is 3. is 4. am 5. are
6. are 7. are

B 1. is 2. is 3. am 4. are
5. is 6. am

C 1. is 2. is 3. is 4. is
5. are 6. are 7. are

Practice 2
▶ 본문 p.154

2. I am thirsty
나 목말라.
3. Today's dinner is curry
오늘 저녁은 카레야.
4. The dessert is in the fridge
디저트는 냉장고에 있어.
5. I am full
나 배불러요.
6. The cafe is on the first floor
그 카페는 1층에 있어.
7. My computer is old
내 컴퓨터는 낡았어.
8. This mobile phone is brand new
이 휴대폰은 신상품이야.
9. Superman and Batman are cartoon characters
슈퍼맨과 배트맨은 만화 캐릭터야.
10. "Zootopia" is the best movie ever
'주토피아'는 역대 최고의 영화야.
11. "Shrek" is the best movie
12. Iron Man is my hero
아이언맨은 내 영웅이야.
13. I am better off alone
나는 혼자 있는 게 나아.
14. They are mad or scared
그들은 화나 있거나 두려워하고 있다.
15. Your dad is so stressed
너의 아빠는 몹시 스트레스를 받으셨어.
16. You are my best friend
네가 나의 최고의 친구야.
17. These penguins are so cute
이 펭귄들은 정말 귀엽다.
18. I am a slow walker

Practice 3
▶ 본문 p.156

2. Dad is in a meeting
아빠는 회의 중이야.
3. I am at home now
나 지금 집에 있어.
4. I am two hours late
난 2시간 늦었어.
5. I am a visitor
난 방문자야.
6. I am a stranger here
나는 여기가 처음이야.
7. The line is busy
통화 중입니다.
8. She is a teacher

그녀는 선생님이야.

9. He is short
그는 키가 작아.

10. My mother[mom] is in the kitchen
내 어머니는 부엌에 계셔.

11. The kids are in the pool
아이들은 수영장에 있어.

12. The final test is around the corner
기말시험이 다가왔어.

13. The holiday is on Friday
휴일은 금요일이야.

14. You are clever
넌 똑똑해.

15. You are a liar
넌 거짓말쟁이야!

16. We are Korean
우리는 한국인이다.

17. My hobby is reading webcomics
내 취미는 웹툰 보는 거야.

18. He is the best basketball player
그는 최고의 농구 선수야.

19. She is my favorite singer
그녀는 내가 가장 좋아하는 가수야.

Let's Practice More!

SET 01 ▶ 본문 p.158

02. are	03. am	04. is
05. are	06. am	07. are
08. is	09. am	10. is
11. is	12. are	

SET 02 ▶ 본문 p.159

02. are	03. are	04. is
05. are	06. is	07. is
08. are	09. is	10. are
11. is	12. is	13. are
14. is		

SET 03 ▶ 본문 p.160

02. is	03. am	04. are
05. is	06. is	07. are
08. is	09. are	10. is
11. are	12. is	13. am
14. are		

SET 04 ▶ 본문 p.161

02. You	03. She	04. I
05. He	06. We	07. They
08. He	09. I	10. You
11. They	12. He	

SET 05 ▶ 본문 p.162

02. She, is	03. He, is	
04. They, are	05. She, is	06. I, am
07. You, are	08. It, is	09. He, is
10. We, are	11. They, are	12. I, am
13. It, is	14. He, is	

SET 06 ▶ 본문 p.163

02. He's	03. She's	04. We're
05. They're	06. She's	07. You're
08. I'm	09. They're	10. He's
11. They're	12. We're	13. I'm
14. It's		

SET 07 ▶ 본문 p.164

02. ~에 있다	03. ~이다	04. ~이다	05. ~이다
06. ~이다	07. ~에 있다	08. ~이다	09. ~에 있다
10. ~이다	11. ~에 있다	12. ~에 있다	13. ~이다
14. ~에 있다	15. ~이다	16. ~이다	17. ~에 있다
18. ~이다	19. ~이다	20. ~에 있다	

SET 08 ▶ 본문 p.165

02. He, is, best	03. They, are, parents
04. dessert, is	05. He, is
06. We, are	07. cafe, is, first
08. I, am, late	09. You, are
10. She, is	11. These, are, cute
12. That, cat, is	13. My, dad[father], is
14. cat, is	15. Vegetables, are
16. I, am	17. He, is
18. They, are	19. She, is
20. kids[children], are	

Chapter 03~05 실전테스트 ▶ 본문 p.166

01. They	02. her	
03. us	04. him	05. ③
06. ①	07. ①	08. ①
09. ②	10. (m)ine	
11. These	12. Those	
13. These	14. That	
15. It is hot summer.	16. It is Sunday morning.	

17. It is April 13th.
18. 인칭대명사: her, us 지시대명사: this, those

19. ②	20. ①	

21. We go to school together.
22. They are on the street.

23. am	24. are	25. is
26. ①	27. ①	28. ②

29. My sister is pretty.
30. You are tall.

ANSWER 핵심 문법 사항

인칭대명사

TEST 1

① my ② mine ③ you ④ yours ⑤ him ⑥ his ⑦ her
⑧ its ⑨ us ⑩ you ⑪ you ⑫ them

TEST 2

1 my **2** he **3** its
4 him **5** Its

TEST 3

1 they **2** you **3** he
4 she **5** it **6** we

명사의 복수형

TEST 4

1 ① -es ② buses ③ boxes ④ churches ⑤ dishes
⑥ -es ⑦ potatoes ⑧ tomatoes ⑨ pianos ⑩ photos
⑪ -s ⑫ radios ⑬ audios

2 ① i ② -es ③ candies ④ countries ⑤ -s ⑥ days
⑦ boys ⑧ v ⑨ -es ⑩ leaves ⑪ wolves ⑫ knives
⑬ roofs

3 ① deer ② fish ③ sheep ④ feet ⑤ teeth ⑥ men
⑦ women ⑧ geese ⑨ mice

Game 정답

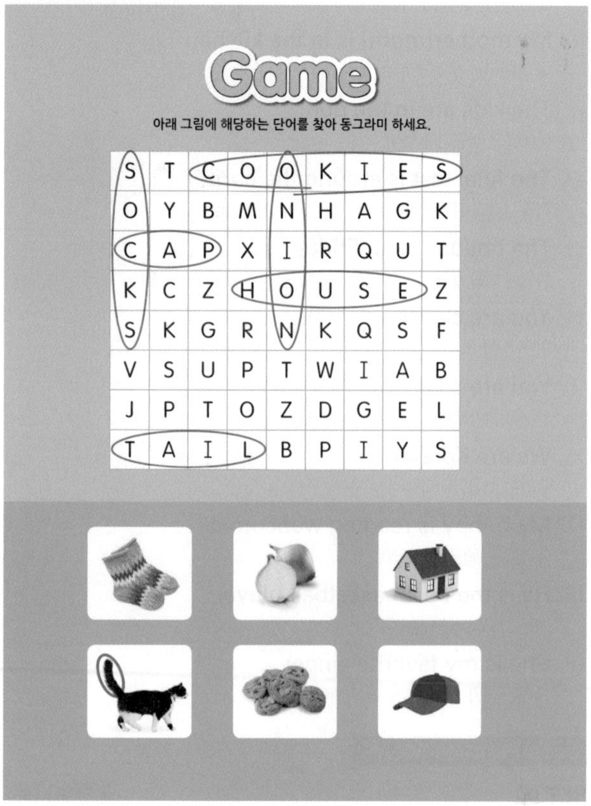

초등영문법 3800제 서평

초등3학년 아이.. 원서는 어느 정도 잘 읽는데.. 글씨 쓰는 걸 많이 어려워해요. 그래서 문법을 알면 도움이 되지 않을까 싶어서 찾다가 3800제를 만났네요. 초등 저학년 아이가 혼자서 하는데 있어서 어려움이 없어요. 쉬운 단어로 설명을 해주니 쉽게 이해하고 공책에 배운 걸 써보기도 하면서 혼자서 열심히 공부하고 있어요. 2번, 3번 쭈욱~~ 3800제로 나갈까 합니다. ***YES24*** / 은**주

형이 중학교 진학 전부터 중학생용 3800제를 풀고 있었고 3800제 구성이 만족스러워서 초등 동생도 풀기 시작했어요. 개념도 구체적이고 다양한 내용이 있어서 좋았어요. 지루하지 않게 그림이 자주 삽입되어 있으니까 덜 삭막해요^^ 무엇보다 각도로 연습문제가 진짜진짜 많아요. 어설프게 알고 진도 나가면 나중에 다시 봤을 때 까먹게 되고 제대로 이해 못하게 되거든요. 다양한 방식의 문제를 풀면서 영어실력이 확장되는 게 느껴져요. 게임, 마크만 성실, 꼼꼼하게 하지 공부는 대충 해치우고 마는 아이인데 이 교재를 통해서 언젠가는 영어 실력이 차곡차곡 쌓이길 기대해봅니다. 뒷편에는 단어 공부, 받아쓰기 연습을 할 수 있는 것도 있어요. 아이 핸드폰에 mp3파일을 넣어주면 스스로 할 수 있겠더라구요. 아직은 진도를 빨리 빼느라 숙제주진 않았는데 방학 시작하면 이 한권으로 영어공부는 충분할 것 같습니다. 핸드폰이 게임, 유튜브 보는 것만이 아닌 공부할 적에도 사용하는 것이라는 것을 알게 되길~^^; ***YES24*** / 희*

잠수네로 별칭되는 엄마표 영어를 한 지 몇 년 되었는데 엄마가 너무 띄엄띄엄 지도하다 보니 아이 단어와 문법이 많이 약한 것 같아 문법 교재로 구매했습니다. Unit 시작할 때 단어가 스물 몇 개 있고 의미를 인지하고 있는지 셀프 테스팅 하도록 구성되어 있고 개념 문제 뒤 연습문제가 쭉 있어서 아이가 스스로 정리하며 공부할 수 있어요. 난이도는 쉬운 편이라 차라리 부담 없이 스르륵 풀 수 있어서 좋아요. ***YES24*** / d**rh0424

문법은 실제로 문장 속에서 활용해봐야 이해가 쉽기 때문에 예제 중심의 반복학습이 가능한 책을 찾다가 선택한 교재입니다. 여러 형식으로 문제 풀이가 다양하게 제시되어 있어 문제를 풀다보면 그 원리가 절로 체득되어 정말 좋습니다. 아직 문법이라는 추상적인 개념을 이해하기 어려워하는 초등학생들에게 좋은 교재예요. 기존에 기초 문법의 틀이 조금 잡혀 있는 학생들은 자습용으로도 좋고 처음 문법을 접하는 학생들에게는 단계적으로 심화되는 문제 구성을 차근차근 밟아가며 공부하기에 좋습니다. ***YES24*** / a**owa

---

아이 문법 학습을 위해서 구입을 하게 되었습니다. 큰아이 중학영문법 3800제를 가지고 학습을 한 경험이 있어 믿고 구입하게 되었는데 역시나 초등문법도 많은 연습문제로 아이들이 같은 내용을 꾸준히 반복 연습하게 구성이 되어있어서 마음에 듭니다. 초등학생용이라 글씨도 큼직큼직하고 페이지마다 빈공간도 많이 있어 답답하지도 않아서 좋아요. 초등학생 아이들은 일단 글씨가 작고 빽빽하면 보면서 질려하는 경향이 있는데 이 교재는 그런 점에서는 후한 점수를 주고 싶네요. 단순 객관식 문제 풀이로 학습시키고 싶은 분들에게는 추천하지 않구요. 객관식 문제풀이가 단원 끝에 단원테스트에 조금 밖에 없어서요. 객관식 문제풀이가 아닌 아이가 문장을 만들면서 학습하기를 원하시는 분들에게는 강추합니다. 타 학습서들이 보통 초등문법을 2권 내지 3권에 끝내는 것을 이 초등영문법 3800제는 1권부터 8권까지에 연습할 부분을 나누어 놓았으니 얼마나 많은 반복을 시킬 수 있는지 권수만 봐도 알 수 있지요. 어쨌든, 초등학교 4학년 아이 8권까지 열심히 공부할 예정입니다. ***YES24*** / j**onim

book.toptutor.co.kr

구하기 어려운 교재는 마더텅 모바일(인터넷)을 이용하세요. 즉시 배송해 드립니다.

마더텅 학습 교재 이벤트에 참여해 주세요. 참여해 주신 모든 분께 선물을 드립니다.

이벤트 1 1분 간단 교재 사용 후기 이벤트

마더텅은 고객님의 소중한 의견을 반영하여 보다 좋은 책을 만들고자 합니다.
교재 구매 후, <교재 사용 후기 이벤트>에 **참여해 주신 모든 분**께는 감사의 마음을 담아 **모바일 문화상품권 1천 원권** 을 보내 드립니다. 지금 바로 QR 코드를 스캔해 소중한 의견을 보내 주세요!

이벤트 2 학습계획표 이벤트

STEP 1 책을 다 풀고 SNS 또는 수험생 커뮤니티에 작성한 학습계획표 사진을 업로드

필수 태그 #마더텅 #초등영어 #초등영문법3800 #학습계획표 #공스타그램
SNS/수험생 커뮤니티 페이스북, 인스타그램, 블로그, 네이버/다음 카페 등

STEP 2 왼쪽 QR 코드를 스캔하여 작성한 게시물의 URL 인증

참여해 주신 모든 분께는 감사의 마음을 담아 **CU 모바일 편의점 상품권 1천 원권** 및 **B 북포인트 2천 점** 을 드립니다.

이벤트 3 블로그/SNS 이벤트

STEP 1 자신의 블로그/SNS 중 하나에 마더텅 교재에 대한 사용 후기를 작성

필수 태그 #마더텅 #초등영어 #초등영문법3800 #교재리뷰 #공스타그램
필수 내용 마더텅 교재 장점, 교재 사진

STEP 2 왼쪽 QR 코드를 스캔하여 작성한 게시물의 URL 인증

참여해 주신 모든 분께는 감사의 마음을 담아 **CU 모바일 편의점 상품권 2천 원권** 및 **B 북포인트 3천 점** 을 드립니다.
매달 우수 후기자를 선정하여 **모바일 문화상품권 2만 원권** 과 **B 북포인트 1만 점** 을 드립니다.

B 북포인트란? 마더텅 인터넷 서점 **http://book.toptutor.co.kr**에서 교재 구매 시 현금처럼 사용할 수 있는 포인트입니다.

※자세한 사항은 해당 QR 코드를 스캔하거나 홈페이지 이벤트 공지글을 참고해 주세요.
※당사 사정에 따라 이벤트의 내용이나 상품이 변경될 수 있으며 변경 시 홈페이지에 공지합니다. ※만 14세 미만은 부모님께서 신청해 주셔야 합니다.
※상품은 이벤트 참여일로부터 2~3일(영업일 기준) 내에 발송됩니다. ※동일 교재로 세 가지 이벤트 모두 참여 가능합니다. (단, 같은 이벤트 중복 참여는 불가합니다.)
※이벤트 기간: 2024년 12월 31일까지 (*해당 이벤트는 당사 사정에 따라 조기 종료될 수 있습니다.)

정답은 뒷면에서 확인하세요.

Find and circle.

그림에 알맞은 단어를 찾아 동그라미 하세요.

1.

p i p g e a p i n k a

2.

m i l c u p i d o d t

3.

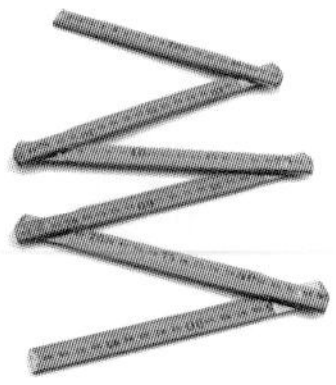

w l z i g z a g p m o

4.

b d i g q x u m i t i

5.

d u b i p y r a m i d

Find and circle.

그림에 알맞은 단어를 찾아 동그라미 하세요.

1. 

p i p g e a (p i n) k a

2. 

m i l (c u p i d) o d t

3. 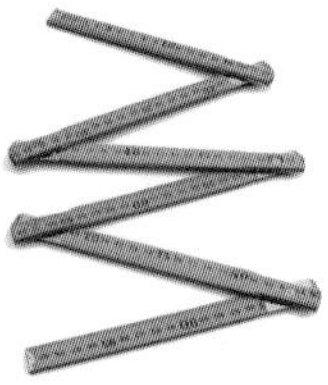

w l (z i g z a g) p m o

4. 

b (d i g) q x u m i t i

5. 

d u b i (p y r a m i d)